DATE DUE

Complete Book of
GOURD CARVING

Jim Widess & Ginger Summit

Sterling Publishing Co., Inc.
New York

Edited by Jeanette Green
Designed by Judy Morgan
Photos by Jim Widess unless otherwise noted

Library of Congress Cataloging-in-Publication Data

Widess, Jim.
    Complete book of gourd carving / Jim Widess & Ginger Summit.
        p. cm.
    Includes index.
    ISBN 1-4027-0442-9
    1. Gourd craft. I. Summit, Ginger. II. Title.
TT873.5.S8597 2004
745.5-dc22   2004003340

2   4   6   8   10 9   7   5   3

Published by Sterling Publishing Co., Inc.
387 Park Avenue South, New York, NY 10016
©2004 by Jim Widess and Ginger Summit
Distributed in Canada by Sterling Publishing
℅ Canadian Manda Group, 165 Dufferin Street
Toronto, Ontario, Canada M6K 3H6
Distributed in Great Britain by Chrysalis Books Group PLC,
The Chrysalis Building, Bramley Road, London W10 6SP, England
Distributed in Australia by Capricorn Link (Australia) Pty. Ltd.
P.O. Box 704, Windsor, NSW 2756, Australia

Manufactured in China
All rights reserved

Sterling ISBN 1-4027-0442-9

For information about custom editions, special sales, premium and
corporate purchases, please contact Sterling Special Sales
Department at 800-805-5489 or specialsales@sterlingpub.com

Caution

Carving tools are sharp and dangerous. Injury can result from the misuse or careless use of chisels, knives, drills, and saws. Sharp tools cause fewer accidents than dull tools. Use common sense, please. The dust resulting from carving gourds contains silica, mold particles, and who knows what else. Eye, nose, mouth, ear, and skin protection should be worn to protect the artist from allergic and toxic reactions. The instructions and tips in this book are the synthesis of our experiences as well as the experiences shared with us by more than 100 gourd carvers across the United States, Canada, and Australia. Your experience may differ, but we hope it will still be a fulfilling and inspiring one. Please direct any questions about gourd crafting to the authors at our e-mail address: jimandginger@caning.com Please write "Gourd Carving" in the subject line.

Decorative Gourd Credits

Front cover (left column, top to bottom): (1) Woodturner's Gourd Bowl, Bob Hosea (2) Celtic Knots, Cass Iverson (3) Maori Motifs, Theo Schoon, New Zealand; collection of Carol Rookstool (4) Desert Jasper, Leah Comerford

Front cover (right column, top to bottom): (1) Expressions 2002, Dyan Mai Peterson (2) Kapu Paru, Jan Seeger (3) Feather Cutouts, Cam Merkle (4) Fretwork Fantasy Bowl with lid, fretwork and alcohol-based wood stain, Howard Swerdloff.

Front cover (center): Spiral Maze, Robert Dillard

Falling Leaves, Marcia Sairanen

Votive Vessel, Ginger Summit

Plumerias, Liza Muhly

CONTENTS

Gourd carving is an ancient art found all over the world.

INTRODUCTION TO GOURD CARVING

$\mathcal{W}$hen traveling around the world, we find many examples of people who have left their mark on a tree, stone, or picnic table. Sometimes we see a name and date. Or maybe it's a random doodle with a knife, a sharp stone, or even a fingernail—whatever is available at that moment of artistic drive. Before we had writing implements, such as ink and quill or the lead/graphite pencil, we made marks in clay tablets. The desire to etch, impress, engrave, incise, and carve has been with us for millennia. Designs created by outlining, stippling, and cross-hatching to depict the real and the imaginary or the sacred and the whimsical are found in every place of human habitation where stones exist or plants grow. Some of the oldest transportable examples of this art form are carvings on gourds.

HISTORY OF GOURD CARVING, BURNING & DECORATION

Humans have used gourds for thousands of years and in all parts of their lives. Although gourds are biodegradable and often fragile, enough evidence has been found to document that gourds were used in nearly every culture and literally every aspect of life. In many cultures, gourds are still frequently used in daily life. We can combine these observations with clues from the past to create vivid details of the story of gourds and humankind.

A mouse carved this gourd from Kemper Stone's crop. All kinds of animals have been known to leave their own distinctive marks on gourds.

Many of the shards and portions of gourds are found in ancient scrap heaps or burial mounds. We know that the lives of the people were difficult, the environment harsh, the tools few. But one fascinating feature is just how many of the gourd remains are decorated and embellished, which suggests that those gourds were not merely a convenience but a canvas as well. Tools available for embellishment were minimal, but the decorated fragments reveal a surprising variety of styles and techniques.

Burning and carving are the two techniques found most often on ancient gourd fragments. The burned gourd shells appear to have been either scorched with acid or embers or marked by a hot tool, such as an arrow or knife. The carved shells are precursors of the gourds found in this book. Ancient gourd shells hold clues, not only about the tools and materials in use at the time of their creation but also about another cultural achievement, the human aesthetic sense of design. Embellished gourds reveal that these ancient cultures valued decoration and dedicated time and resources to its accomplishment. Ancient carved gourds provide insight into the evolution and refinement of tools and techniques as well as into people's social roles, activities, belief systems, and relationship to the world around them.

Gourd Carving in Peru

For more than 4,500 years, Peru has been home to gourd artists and craftsmen. The types of decoration on these ancient fragments include scratching on the outer shell, fine-line hatching, and a combination of pyroengraving and carving. Interestingly, gourds have been in continuous use in Peru since that time, and although specific designs and details have changed, contemporary artists still retain many of the motifs found on these prehistoric remnants.

Gourd images provide a fascinating historical record of many features of daily life through the centuries. Religious ceremonies and beliefs, political events, and social activities are all illustrated in exqui-

Ancient Cat, Tito Medina. Using traditional hand-carving tools and scorching, Medina copied the feline image from an ancient Peruvian gourd. The original artifact is in the collection of Museo de la Cultura Peruana in Lima, Peru.

Pelicans. This shallow gourd bowl from the Chimu culture of the north coast of Peru was made between 1400 and 1000 B.C. It is inlaid outside with abalone shell chips forming a frieze of pelicans with fish in their beaks. On the bowl's bottom are numerous small abalone circles enclosed by a large circle. It is also inlaid with spondylus shell. Courtesy of the Tucson Museum of Art.

site detail on gourds. After European contact, paints and dyes were added to native decorative techniques, but in Peru, carving has remained the most popular form of gourd embellishment.

Today, although most gourds are grown in Peru's coastal areas where abundant water and hot, dry temperatures prevail, the villages with the most gourd-carving families are in the mountains to the south-east. Regular trade routes provide raw gourds to the mountain craftspeople, and the finished objects are delivered to market destinations, such as Cuzco, Lima-Callao, and the coast.

The distinctive decorative styles used by Peruvian carvers tend to be traditional to each village, culture, or family. For example, the Huanta area is well-known for the sugar-bowl gourd carved with intricate scenes of daily life. The outlines are carved with a burin or sharpened nail, and then charcoal is rubbed in to reveal the designs.

The designs created around the town of Huancayo show indigenous Indian rather than Spanish influence. Most often the artist scorches a selected area and then carves or inscribes the design, again using a burin. Instead of rubbing in charcoal to darken the cut lines, often the artist uses chalk to make the carved areas lighter. Another innovation used in this region is the technique of dyeing the whole gourd and then carving the design.

The gourds carved around Ayacucho are first scorched to give a black or dark brown background that contrasts with the light, carved, soft inner shell.

Gourd plate carved with detailed scenes of daily life, Peru. Collection of Kathryn Westfall.

Peace Corps volunteers introduced an innovation that turns bulbous small gourds into sculptural objects, such as birds, animals, or fish. These are now popular tourist items, and they may incorporate many other carving techniques.

Village Farm Life, Tito Medina. This snake gourd was burned to create depth and whitened with calcium. The contemporary Peruvian artist draws on traditional themes.

Gourd Carving in Oceania

Gourds were used for many different functions in daily life on Pacific islands stretching from the Philippines to Hawaii. Although many locations did not have enough soil to grow gourds, they were often obtained through trade and embellished with designs specific to each locale.

On many Pacific islands, betel nuts are used to produce a slightly intoxicating effect when the nut is peeled and chewed with a bit of lime (obtained from crushed lime or shells). Traditionally, gourd containers of a wide variety of shapes and sizes have been used to hold the lime powder as well as other sacred powders and ingredients for ceremonies.

Lime container, Papua, New Guinea. Collection of Ginger Summit.

Lime container, Papua, New Guinea.
Collection of Ginger Summit.

Shaman's neck pouch, East Timor, Indonesia. Collection of Virginia Saunders.

Lime container, Melanesia.
Collection of Ginger Summit.

In Hawaii and other South Pacific islands, the faces of warriors often were covered with tattoos and scarification patterns which revealed not only their own identity but that of their family and ancestors. To perhaps hide this information during certain ceremonies, rituals, or functions, islanders wore masks made of gourds or basketry. Captain Cook remarked on this distinctive headgear in his journals in the 1700s.

Hawaiian gourd mask, artist Emiko Matsutsuyu.

Maori Gourd Carving in New Zealand

The Maori's use of gourds has been well documented since they settled in New Zealand in the 12th century. The original settlers, of Polynesian origin, carried supplies for trading and establishing settlements on long ocean voyages. Many ocean-going supplies were packed in gourd containers. Gourd vessels were also used to bail water out of canoes, buoy nets as floats, and serve as eating utensils.

Museum displays in Auckland and Wellington feature gourds of many different shapes, sizes, and types, including bottle, bushel, kettle, long snakelike, and dipper gourds with thick necks of varying lengths. The Maori, exceptionally talented wood carvers, applied this skill to gourds as well. The designs were very specific to their culture. All design elements carried meaning, and only certain combinations were allowed on different shapes of gourds. Carved gourds were usually reserved for nobility or for specific ceremonies, and the details within the designs often identified the owner.

One New Zealand artist, Theo Schoon, who was not Maori, is recognized as a master gourd carver in the Maori tradition. Born in Indonesia to Dutch parents, Schoon attended art school in Europe and moved to New Zealand in the 1940s. In his research of rock carving, he became very interested in the designs applied to gourd surfaces. Because gourds had been largely neglected in New Zealand in recent times, Schoon began to grow his own gourds and apprenticed himself to a Maori master carver to perfect his skills.

Although Theo Schoon carved gourds daily for 8 to 10 years, most were sold to tourists, and only a few examples remain in museum collections. We know his work through articles that appeared in art magazines and exhibitions as well as through his abundant correspondence that describes his fascination with growing and carving gourds. Virginia Umberger, a gourd artist and grower in Illinois, was one correspondent. His letters provide great insight not only into growing gourds of good quality but also into Maori carving traditions.

This gourd was carved in Maori traditional motifs by Theo Schoon. Collection of Virginia Umberger.

Gourd Carving in Africa

Although gourds are used throughout the African continent for largely the same purposes and functions, widely different traditions exist regarding embellishment. In many African cultures, however, some gourds are decorated to enhance a special function or role, such as providing a bride's dowry, service for a king or great leader, or as part of a ceremony or ritual. Each culture or tribal group developed a unique style and technique for decorating these special gourds. While small variations of the design may be created by the individual artist or varied to fit the particular shape and size of gourd, the overall styles remain identifiable to specific geographic areas or groups of people.

One frequently used technique is similar to engraving in other parts of the world. With a small sharp tool, the artist scratches the design into a freshly dried shell. Then he rubs the entire gourd with a mixture of ash and grease to darken the scratched patterns.

Detail of Theo Schoon's Maori motifs.

This canteen reflects the European dress and patterns of 19th century Europe, and it was used in the Boer Wars in southern Africa. Collection of Ginger Summit.

Gourd container from Kenya.
Collection of Virginia Saunders.

*Gourd fragment from
Cameroon.* Collection of
Ginger Summit.

Bowl from Burkina Faso. Collection of Ginger Summit.

In another technique, the artist uses a wider chisel type of tool to carve away larger portions of the gourd shell to fashion a design or to create a contrast to other designs carved in the shell. Often the soft exposed inner shell is rubbed with chalk to intensify the contrast with the smooth outer shell.

A large carving tool, similar to a sharp wedge, created the pattern with a combination of deep grooves on this Nigerian gourd. The finer lines are pressure engraved; the artist uses an iron point embedded in a handle, which is pushed across the gourd's surface to create combinations of lines, cross-hatching, and notches.

The background of this gourd from Kenya was removed around an elaborate animal motif. Collection of Ginger Summit.

A technique using similar tools in Nigeria results in deeply carved wedges and grooves in a gourd shell from which the outer epidermis has been removed. These gourds are intended for decorative purposes only, so that often cuts go completely through the gourd. Rubbing the surface with chalk, pencil lead, or charcoal can enhance the design.

Nigerian deeply carved gourd with cutouts and charcoal.
Collection of Dick and Beanie Wezelman.

Nigeria.   Collection of Ginger Summit.

Nigeria.   Collection of the author.

This elaborately carved, covered container is from the Yoruba people of Nigeria. A variety of chisel and knife techniques are used to create the overall bird motif. (See pp. 85–86 for more details about the technique.)
Courtesy of the Phoebe Apperson Hearst Museum of Anthropology and the regents of the University of California at Berkeley. Photo by Terèse Babineau, catalog #5-15649a,b.

Gourd Carving in China

For thousands of years in China, gourds, embellished with a wide variety of techniques, have been used for many purposes. Needle engraving is a popular form of carving that's used primarily to decorate small egg-shaped gourds with thin shells. With a sharp needle, the artist scratches the design onto the surface of the gourd, which is then carefully inked. The designs frequently depict scenes from nature, such as mountains, trees, clouds, and ocean. Such scenes are embellished with details of birds or other small animals. Other topics are people in serene settings or figures from mythology.

Scholar gourd, China.
Collection of the author.

Scholar gourd, China.
Collection of Norma A. Fox.

FINDING THE RIGHT TOOLS

Many different kinds of tools can be used to carve gourds, including most of those made for cutting and shaping wood. This includes all varieties of saws, knives, gouging tools, and chipping blades. Artists also have adapted tools from other crafts, such as scrimshaw blades and utensils made for shaping ceramics and pottery. Even dental tools are handy for finishing many gourd carvings. Gourd shells vary in thickness and density, so some heavier tools designed for wood may be unsuitable for many gourds and cause them to crack or chip.

Since the field of hobby wood crafting and carving remains popular, lots of tools are designed and marketed to suit specific materials. These smaller tools intended for detail work or hobby crafting are ideal for gourd enthusiasts. Many tools, such as keyhole saws, chisels, sanding blocks, files, etc., may already be part of your household tool supply. Craft and hardware stores usually carry inexpensive sets of attachments for hobby knife handles, including saw blades, carving blades, and gouges. If you already have these common tools on hand, you'll be able to explore with little expense new ways to carve gourds.

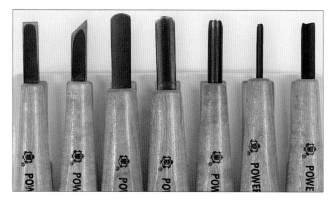

This inexpensive introductory set of seven chisels and gouges includes a #1 7-mm flat chisel, a #2 10-mm skew chisel, a #3 8-mm straight gouge, a #6 8-mm straight gouge, a #8 6-mm straight gouge, a #10 2-mm straight gouge, and a #39 6-mm V-tool. (The first number is the sweep or "smile" of the chisel or gouge, and the second number is its millimeter width.)

After you get started, however, you'll find that stores and catalogs specializing in wood-carving supplies offer a huge variety of specialty hand and power tools to meet every need and budget. Because some tools represent a sizeable investment, select them with care. Consider not only the shape, size, and quality of the blade but also how the handle fits in your hand. There are many styles of carving, and the shape of the handle and technique used for cutting will be important to your wrist and arm muscles.

A Note About Chisels & Gouges

When you buy chisels and gouges, remember that the number preceded by the "#" represents the "sweep" or the "smile" of the chisel, and the second number represents the millimeter width of the cutting edge of the tool. The terms *flat chisel, skew chisel, straight gouge,* and *V-tool* describe the shape of the blade's working edge.

Sharpening Hand Tools

How to sharpen hand-carving tools is an important skill to learn. A dull blade is both inefficient and potentially dangerous. It will cut the gourd less effectively, and when the artist pushes harder to do the job, the blade may skip or cut beyond the intended line. While stone has traditionally been used for sharpening, other materials, such as ceramic and diamond also work well. Sharpening stones come in many different grits, and sharpening kits are available with two or more different grits or compositions of stone. Usually water or oil is necessary to lubricate the stone as you are sharpening so that the grit of the stone doesn't get clogged. The manufacturer will recommend the best lubricant.

Gouges come in many different curvatures, but the cutting edge requires sharpening just as does any other blade. It is possible to hold the gouge and gently rock it back and forth on a flat surface while sharpening the outer surface. Rounded or profiled slip stones are

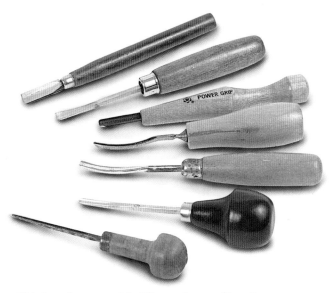

Chisels and gouges with different shapes of handles.

specially designed to accommodate both the inside and the exterior edges of the different curvatures and are available wherever these tools are sold.

Be sure to keep a sharpening stone set with your tools, and remember to use it. New Zealand artist Theo Schoon stated that one of the most valuable lessons he learned from the Maori carvers was to sharpen tools often—many times during the day. Not only do sharp edges make the carving process easier, but they make the tools much safer as well.

Traditional handmade tools and natural sharpening stone, owned by Julio Seguil Ríos of Cuzco, Peru.

Sharpening stones (left to right): Japanese water stone, oil-stone, sharpening oil, profile stone, and Arkansas stone.

POWER TOOLS

The broad spectrum of power carving tools can be divided into categories according to three types of stroke or movement of the cutting blade: (1) the jigsaw, (2) the scroll saw, and (3) the rotary carver.

Jigsaws

One type of power carving tool involves a reciprocating up-and-down movement of a saw blade that's commonly identified as a jigsaw. While some jigsaws designed for general woodworking can be used on large, thick-shelled gourds, they are usually too heavy for smaller gourds. The blade itself is often thick. The teeth, designed for ripping wood, produce a wide rough cut in gourd shells, and the reciprocating up-and-down motion of the blade often cracks the shell of dry or brittle gourds.

Several smaller models of jigsaws designed for the hobby market are perfect for gourd crafting. They typically come with a power transformer, which has a dial for adjusting the saw blade's speed. These saws have become extremely popular for use with all but the thickest of gourd shells. It's important to keep in mind that these saws were designed to cut relatively soft materials such as balsa wood. Thin-shelled and medium-shelled gourds are ideal for these saws, but the saws often have problems cutting through dense, thicker shells. Just remember not to push or force the blade while cutting. This may cause the blade to bend slightly and either bind or break. Although it's easy to replace the blades, forcing the cut puts undue pressure on the motor and may cause it to burn out. If you remember to cut slowly, and to stop and back up slightly if the motor begins to labor, the hobby saw can be a versatile and valuable aid to gourd carving.

Scroll Saws

A second type of tool with a reciprocating saw blade is a hobby scroll saw. This type of tool has largely been neglected by the gourd crafting community, probably because gourds have too much bulk for this kind of tool. However, it is an excellent choice when carving pieces of shell. If the shard is relatively flat, the design can be drawn on the exterior shell and cut with that side up. If the shard is larger and has more curvature, draw the design on the interior shell, and cut with the shell upside down—that is, with the exterior shell against the saw table.

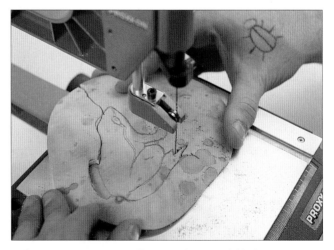

Seth Rittweger uses a scroll saw with a spiral blade to cut out this frog from a gourd scrap.

Artist Seth Rittweger makes animal cutouts from pieces of gourd shells.

Rotary Carvers

The third, very popular, category of power carving tool is the rotary carver. These tools are based on the concept of a drill: the end of the handheld device grips a cutting burr or bit, which rotates at high speeds to grind away portions of the gourd shell. Many models within this broad category feature miniature motors that are housed directly within the handheld casing. While suitable for small tasks, after carving for any length of time they tend to get heavy and awkward to maneuver. To overcome this problem, manufacturers created a flexible shaft that can be attached to the motor unit. With the flexible-shaft extension, you can brace the tool on a table or hanging support while holding the small hand piece at the end of the shaft that grips the bits with a collet or chuck.

There are two basic styles of house-voltage power carvers, differing in the general shape of motor unit.

One style, designed to be held in the hand while carving, has a cylindrical housing with the small motor inside. The other style of rotary carver does not attempt to enclose the motor in a handheld device; instead, the motor is contained in a larger separate housing with a flexible shaft to hold the bits. Because these models are not handheld, the motors can be more powerful. This style of rotary carver can operate at up to 35,000 rpm.

Rotary carvers powered by an air compressor are becoming increasingly popular among gourd crafters. These pneumatic tools can achieve an extremely high rpm, ranging from 300,000 to 500,000 rpm, and can carve gourd shells with ease and precision. Some brands will accommodate a variety of bit shanks, while others are constructed to only hold 1/16-inch shanks. Often the bits used by dentists fit these tools, available either through

You can use a Gourd Drill with a ball-tip burr to remove background.

dental-supply catalogs or from your dentist when he replaces his tools. The heads of bits made for pneumatic drills are often extremely fine, allowing for very detailed lines and etching.

In addition to the flexible-shaft attachment, which many artists consider essential, the foot pedal control allows greater flexibility in controlling both the speed and the motor's power switch. This is particularly useful for those tools with controls in an awkward place, such as away from your hand's usual position.

Bits & Burrs, Cutters & Engravers

Hobby stores and catalogs stock a large variety of bits that can be used with all the rotary power tools described above. High-speed cutting bits have two main parts—the *shaft* (also called the shank), which fits into the rotary tool, and the *head* or tip, which can be made of many different materials and in varying shapes and surfaces. The shafts come in several diameters; the ⅟₁₆ inch, ⅛ inch, and ³⁄₃₂ inch are the most common and will fit most power tools except for some pneumatic carvers. (See Guide to High-Speed Grinder Burrs & Tips, pp. 184–185.)

Some models of handheld carvers require special collets or collars to accommodate different sizes of shafts; others have chucks that can be adjusted and tightened regardless of shank diameter. An adjustable, keyless chuck, for easier changing of cutting bits, is available for high-speed drills that come with collets. (Collets provide a more secure grip of the shank of the cutter when a lot of torque is required, which is usually not the case with gourds.)

Rotary carvers are designed for use with materials as diverse as metals, glass, stone, plastics, and all varieties of wood. Because these materials have a wide range of density and surfaces, bits are available in different compositions; the three most common are carbide steel, tungsten carbide, and diamond-coated steel. All bits can be used effectively with gourds since gourd shells tend to be much softer than most other materials. Like other kinds of blades, cutters tend to get dull after lots of use or misuse. Because there is no efficient way to sharpen them, they simply need to be replaced from time to time.

The heads of the bits come in many shapes and sizes. We can divide them into a few general categories: ball-tip, cylinder with a flat end, bull-nose, cylinder with a rounded end, taper, cone, inverted cone, pear, and flame. Within these categories, the heads come in many diameters and variations in shapes to meet specific carving needs and to fit tools by different manufacturers.

We can also define bits by their function: grinding, cutting, etching, sanding, and polishing. Because gourd shells are relatively soft, bits intended for one function may work quite adequately for other uses as well. For example, coarse sanding drums can be effective for grinding away relatively large amounts of shell.

Bits also come in different compositions and textures: stone, rubber, wire brush, and with different types of grooves. A bit designed for rapid grinding, called the Kutzall or Typhoon surface, looks much like a hedgehog, with small prongs or teeth extending out from a central core. While the bit makes quick work of carving through large areas, it may be too coarse for soft gourd inner shells. The more popular cutting bits made of tungsten and carbide steel have several different patterns of grooves, but they're extremely adaptable for a wide variety of shaping in gourd design. Typically diamond, ruby, or sapphire burrs are available in a variety of shapes with coarse to fine grits; these bits are especially useful for smoothing and texturing.

Bits designed for sanding come in many different materials and shapes. Some have a removable sand-paper cylinder or cap sleeve mounted on a rubber foundation. The sandpaper comes in several different grits, and when it gets clogged or worn after much use, simply remove and replace it. Other sanding bits, which can be used for final texturing, are made of stone or aluminum oxide.

Rotary tool kits often contain an assortment of bits to encourage the user to become familiar with the tool's wide range of uses. Additional bits are available in sets; beginners should look for a set that includes a wide range of shapes. Experiment to find the bits most appropriate for your own carving styles. After you identify the most useful shapes and materials, you can buy bits individually.

SAFETY FIRST, LAST & ALWAYS

When carving gourds, artists should adopt strict safety and health precautions that may not be as critical in other gourd-crafting situations.

Three separate matters to consider are (1) the hazards inherent in the gourd itself, (2) the challenges in working with sharp tools and power tools, and (3) the precautions to follow when working with materials such as dyes, glues, resins, and finishes.

Follow all these precautions whether you're using power tools or hand tools.

▥ *Be aware of the dangers of gourd dust.* Even though people have used gourds for thousands of years, many things are still unknown about them. We

---

SAFETY FIRST

Always use eye protection, a dust mask, and efficient ventilation when using motorized carving accessories. Make sure that carving burrs do not overheat, buried in the material. That's the quickest way to wear out the cutting edge. Instead, frequently lift the burr away from the gourd and allow it to cool while spinning at high speed. In addition, the Dremel manufacturer suggests: "For best results, insert the accessory bit all the way into the tool and then back it out slightly before tightening down. This provides plenty of shank for the collet or chuck to hold onto. Secure objects to a stable surface while working. Use the sides of the cutter, rather than the tip, for effective engraving. The tip cuts poorly and can break under pressure. Use higher speeds for wood. If chattering occurs, increase speed."

---

do know that all parts of the gourd have been used for medicinal purposes by cultures around the globe, but we still do not fully understand the exact chemistry and biology that made these practices effective. Even so, it is important to recognize that certain properties in the gourd itself can cause different kinds of reactions within the body. Some people work with gourds for decades with no ill effect, but others notice allergic reactions in both the respiratory system and on skin. Carving gourds creates a great deal of dust. The particles contain finely ground shell, and any molds present on the exterior or interior surfaces are suddenly pulverized and released into the air.

▥ *Wear gloves for tasks like cleaning and dyeing.* When cleaning, sanding, dyeing, polishing, or varnishing gourds, remember to wear lightweight rubber gloves. You'll find them in most drug or hardware stores sold in boxes of 100. Many artists find that the mold on dirty gourds is irritating to the skin when they scrub or sand the exterior or scrape the interior. Heavy-duty rubber gloves designed for household chores can solve several issues at once. In addition to protecting the hands, the textured rubber provides a good gripping surface to hold the gourd steady as you scrape away stubborn epidermis or pulp.

■ *Always wear a protective glove when carving.* Always wear a protective glove on the hand holding the gourd, especially since the carving knife or gouge often seems aimed directly at this hand. Many styles of glove can be appropriate. Lightweight garden gloves offer some protection, and because they often have a textured rubber surface on the palm, they help hold the gourd secure. Leather gloves designed for bikers or golfers have a comfortable snug fit, protecting the base of the fingers and thumb, and leave the fingertips exposed. An excellent choice is a glove made of Spectra or other material woven with stainless steel. This glove, specially designed for woodcarvers, offers the greatest protection. Whatever your choice, be sure to find a glove that's comfortable and then wear it.

The Razaire filtered exhaust system can be used on the lap or on a work surface. The fan has an adjustable speed control, and several filters can be stacked to provide more or less dust filtration as needed.

■ *Ventilate your work area.* When working with power tools, ventilation is most important. I always carve outside when using power tools. During rainy weather, I work in the garage with the door open and a fan blowing. If you do work indoors, try to have a space where the dust can be captured and evacuated. Simply blowing it away from the face with a fan does not resolve the problem since that causes dust particles to be dispelled throughout the rest of the room or house. If you work indoors, one solution is to use an exhaust system. Many models are available for crafters and include a work tray or box connected by a large vent to a filtered exhaust fan. A good exhaust system can eliminate most of the smoke and dust from your work and immediate environment.

■ *Always wear a mask.* Many styles of dust masks and respirators are on the market today, beginning with the simple dust or particle masks available in most drug, hobby, or hardware stores. While useful for some quick tasks, many of these masks provide minimal protection. That's because they do not form a good seal around the face, and some gourd dust may still enter the nose and mouth. Many artists complain that these masks fog up their glasses, an inconvenience and an indication of the poor seal around the face and nose. A variety of this style of mask is slightly larger and covers more of the face and chin, providing slightly better protection. Some models have an exhalation valve to prevent glasses from fogging.

▨ *Find the right respirator.* Many larger styles of respirators available in hardware and hobby shops are lightweight, usually with adjustable straps to keep the rubber seal secure against the face. These are designed with one or more ventilator holes with filters. If possible, try on a variety of masks to find one that best fits your face. If a mask is not comfortable, you may not choose to wear it, despite good intentions. But it's very important that you do. It is a good idea to buy extra filters and establish a routine to change them. (Respirators work just like your vacuum cleaner: they cannot do the job with a clogged filter.) Gourd artist Marguerite Smith recommends using a face mask commonly used by woodworkers, one with a face plate with a built-in fan at the top to blow dust and smoke away from the face. It does not fog up and is quite comfortable to wear.

Here are two styles of respirator.

▨ *Don't forget to use a fan.* In addition to wearing a mask and working outside, I still have a small fan positioned to blow air away from my face. The added bonus is that the fan also blows dust away from the gourd surface, which allows you to see what you are doing as you carve or sand.

▨ *Find ways to secure the gourd.* Using hand carving tools on gourds presents unique challenges for the

---

SPECIAL NOTE ABOUT POWER TOOLS

Wear earplugs. Power carving tools, including the air-turbine carver, create a noise that can seriously threaten hearing. Fortunately, most drug stores carry many excellent models of earplugs. Find a comfortable style, and keep some in your toolbox. Then make it a practice to always wear them when you turn on power tools.

artist. These tools are principally designed to work with soft, flat wood. Besides being round, gourd shells can be hard and slippery. When carving a gourd, you need to resolve two separate issues: (1) how to hold the gourd secure and (2) how to protect the supporting hand. Whether you brace the gourd on a work surface or on your lap, the gourd will be far more secure if nestled on a rubberized surface. This can be a foam rubber pad or a rubber mat. Even a pad that holds small rugs in place will do, if folded into a small work pad. After nicking a pair of work jeans, I now always wear a leather apron if I am working with the gourd in my lap.

SAFETY NOTE

Always apply leather dyes and spray finishes **outdoors** *or in a well-ventilated area. The solvents in these products can be toxic and must be handled with care.*

CHOOSING & PREPARING GOURDS

Finding the Right Gourd for Your Project

Before you select a gourd, consider how you want to use the finished project as well as the type of carving you want to do.

▨ *Examine the gourd's shape, size, and surface.* For carving, look for a surface that's as even and free from blemishes as possible. While bumps and other irregularities may be a real bonus for other types of embellishment, such as pyrography, they may indicate problems within the shell itself, such as density and thickness. It is harder to carve even lines or patterns on an uneven surface. If the shell is dirty or covered with mold, feel it carefully in your search for a smooth, even shell.

▨ *Consider the shell's density and thickness.* The gourd shell's density and thickness are two separate concerns. Density refers to the firmness of the shell itself. Often a very thin shell may be extremely dense and strong. A thick shell can also be soft and pithy, and easily crumble or break. For carving projects, it is important to try to find a very dense shell, regardless of its thickness. It is hard to determine this quality, and it simply takes experience working with many gourd shells to make this judgment. Even the most experienced gourd artists are often fooled once they actually cut into the shell.

▨ *Is the gourd's shell thick or thin?* For some types of carving, a thin shell will be the most appropriate. For others, you'll want to look for the thickest shell possible. When inspecting a whole gourd, it isn't always easy to figure out the shell's thickness; even very experienced gourd artists may be surprised. Many styles of open fretwork hold up best with dense but thin shells. For engraving, the shell can be thick or thin. Carving techniques that require removing greater amounts of external shell obviously require a thicker shell. A soft or pithy shell, no matter how thick, may not be able to hold a sharp edge when carved and could simply crumble as your work proceeds.

Cleaning the Gourd

To clean a gourd, soak it in warm water for up to 15 minutes; then scrub away the mildew on the outer epidermis. Stubborn spots often remain stuck to the shell's exterior, and these can be scraped away with a dull kitchen knife. Some artists soak stubbornly layered gourds in a very mild solution of detergent or TSP for longer periods and find that the epidermis is easier to remove.

Select a gourd with an even shell.

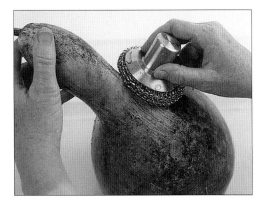

Soak the gourd in warm water. Then remove the mold with a metal kitchen scouring pad.

Removing the Top

To cut the top from a gourd, first draw a line around the neck or wherever you want the opening. Make a cut on the line with a hobby knife or a thin kitchen knife.

Then use a handsaw or power jigsaw to cut along the line. If you are using a power jigsaw, hold the gourd secure with one hand, and then keep the plate of the jigsaw snug against the surface of the gourd. If the jigsaw plate is raised, the saw may knock against the gourd and cause the shell to split, or the blade may bend and break. Although blades are easy to replace, it is good to get in the habit of safe cutting practices.

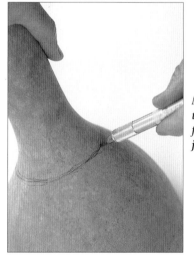

Make an incision along the line you have drawn for insertion of the mini-jigsaw blade.

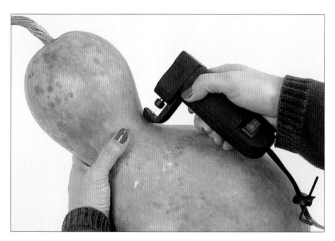

Use the Gourd Saw to cut along the pencil line.

Removing the Pulp

Clean the inside pulp from the gourd, using any tools that you have handy in the kitchen or garage. Specialty tools are available that may be just the thing for hard-to-reach surfaces. Many artists are sensitive to the dust particles released when cleaning the inner pulp. In addition to wearing a mask, they spray the gourd's interior with water or swish water inside the gourd and dump it out.

Long-handled scrapers are a good choice for containers with a small opening.

When it is important to thoroughly clean the interior surface, a kitchen scrubber attached to a long spindle is very helpful. When this is inserted in a drill, the rotating scrubber completely cleans the interior pulp and leaves a smooth surface. This method will raise a lot of gourd dust, so be sure to do this with plenty of ventilation and eyes, nose, and mouth protection. Set the variable speed drill at a very low speed.

Sanding

Some artists like to sand the gourd's exterior surface with fine-grade wet/dry sandpaper. This ensures that all the epidermis is removed and gives the working surface a nice finish. As soon as the gourd is completely clean inside and out, it is ready for carving.

Gourds grown in molds or impressed with a stamp or blunt knife remain uncut and intact.

IMPRESSED GOURDS

IN CHINA

The technique of creating impressed gourds is not technically carving because the gourd shell is not actually cut in the process. Instead it is pressed down, or impressed.

For centuries, artists in ancient China used an agate, ivory, or jade tool to push into, or compress, the gourd's surface with a design. As Wang Shixiang describes in the book, *The Charms of the Gourd*, this technique requires great skill. The oldest impressed gourds may have a purple or yellow tint that indicates the artist, time period, or location of the gourd's creation. Some artists in China today continue to use the impression technique but prefer a steel blade to the more traditional stone or ivory blades.

Sketching the Design

Artists Leigh Adams and Julius Wang describe the technique. First, the artist sketches the design onto the clean, dry gourd shell. Then he outlines the boldest lines with the blade. He holds the tool with the sharper edge against the line and slanted upward so that he can depress the gourd's shell along the lines of the pattern. With the side of the blade, he smoothes out the design's contours, and using another tool with a long, slender blade, he adds fine lines.

Because the texture of gourds varies, the pressure required to make this impression or indentation also varies with each gourd. The most important element of impressing is not to incise the surface. The gourd shell is never actually cut, and no part of the shell is removed. The resulting design is often very soft and somewhat blurred. This technique is very difficult to use with solid gourd shells. Soaking the gourd in water or silicon oil helps soften it.

Ceramic & Plaster Molds for Growing Gourds

Artist Ban Nong jade-knife carved this gourd; detail of impressed design from a gourd planted and molded by Zhang Cairi and Zhang Gang. Gourd Island Gourd Society, Liaoning, China.

This gourd was grown in a mold with no design on the surface. The gourd was planted and molded by Zhang Cairi and Zhang Gang. Gourd Island Gourd Society, Liaoning, China.

This gourd, grown in the same mold, has been embellished with a design impressed in the surface. Zhang Cairi and Zhang Gang planted and molded the gourd, and artist Ban Nong carved it with a jade knife. Gourd Island Gourd Society, Liaoning, China.

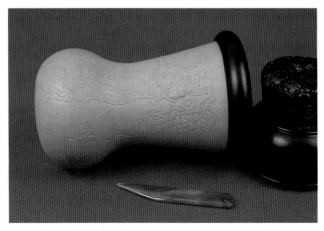

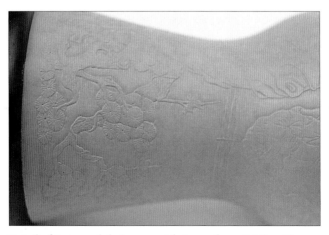

Grown in a mold for a cricket cage, this gourd has been impressed using the agate knife shown by Ban Nong. Gourd Island Gourd Society, Liaoning, China.

Detail of impressed design on cricket cage by artist Ban Nong. Gourd Island Gourd Society, Liaoning, China.

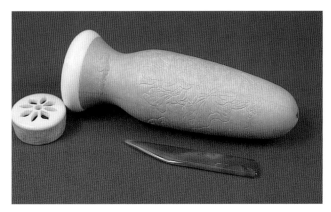

Artist Ban Nong's cricket cage has an impressed design enhanced with the agate blade shown. Gourd Island Gourd Society, Liaoning, China.

This lidded container, made from a molded gourd, reveals an impressed surface design made with the agate blade shown. The gourd was planted and molded by Zhang Cairi and Zhang Gang and jade-knife carved by Ban Nong. Gourd Island Gourd Society, Liaoning, China.

To enhance design details of gourds grown in ceramic or plaster molds, an artist uses a stone blade. Over centuries of practice, the Chinese have perfected this technique, and molds have been designed to create gourds with very complex shapes and combinations of containers with tops. Molds were originally ceramic, made from casts of ornately carved wood designs. Today they're usually plaster and secured around a small growing gourd. When the gourd reaches maturity, the grower opens the mold. However, the design on the gourd's surface may appear somewhat blurred. The gourd artist can use an agate blade to go over outlines and details of the design to enhance the contrasts. Again, no part of the gourd's surface is cut or removed in this process.

This gourd was grown in a mold that had a reverse design on the interior surface. Once the gourd was fully mature, it was removed from the mold. The gourd was planted and molded by Zhang Cairi and Zhang Gang.
Gourd Island Gourd Society, Liaoning, China.

Ban Nong enhanced the outline of the design using an agate blade.
Gourd Island Gourd Society, Liaoning, China.

Design detail enhances the gourd's body. Gourd Island Gourd Society, Liaoning, China.

Note the design detail on the neck of the gourd. Gourd Island Gourd Society, Liaoning, China.

These exquisite molded and jade-knife enhanced gourds were planted and molded by Zhang Cairi and Zhang Gang; Ban Nong jade-knife carved them. Gourd Island Gourd Society, Liaoning, China. Collection of Leigh Adams and Sher Elliott-Widess.

IN SURINAME

Glass Shards Impressed in the Calabash

The Maroons, who live in the Suriname rain forest (formerly Dutch Guiana) of South America, use a similar technique. Although the Maroons grow both the vine gourd and the tree gourd, which they call calabash, they decorate only the calabash. Vine gourds are used for many functions in daily life, but the decorated calabash is considered essential for ceremonial, religious, or social events. With chisels and knives, men decorate the gourd's exterior surface, and women use glass shards to traditionally embellish the gourd's interior.

After they cut open the calabash, they use knives and sandstone to smooth the edges. With the pulp removed, the calabash's interior is usually quite smooth. An artist roughly sketches a design on the interior surface. Then she presses a piece of glass along the lines of the design, creating a sharp edge that tapers slightly away from the design. When she completes the design, she soaks the calabash for up to a week; then she allows it to dry. If rubbed with an abrasive leaf, the design stands out as a slightly darkened pattern.

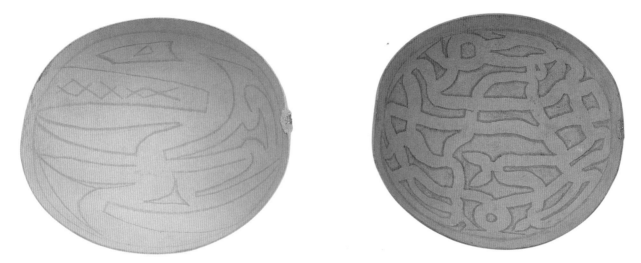

Calabash bowl from Suriname, showing design impressed on the interior surface. Collection of Ginger Summit.

*M*old forming on green gourds may create natural patterns on the shells.

GREEN GOURDS

$\mathcal{T}$he gourd family, *Cucurbitaceae*, has 114 genera, including pumpkins, squashes, gourds, melons, watermelon, cucumbers, gherkins, and chayote, all grown for their edible fruit.

Unlike most fruits, however, those of the *Lagenaria siceraria* (the calabash) dry with hard shells in a huge variety of shapes and sizes, much to the fascination of gourd lovers. Seeds planted in the spring become huge sprawling vines, producing many fruits throughout the summer months. While it is tempting to pick them "when they are just the right size," most gourd enthusiasts know that the fruits must be fully mature before they are harvested.

The best indication of maturity is that the plant's stem is brown and dries at least six inches from the gourd's bulb. Wait until the entire vine has died back, usually by late fall, before gathering in the plants. Although the vines are brown and withered, the gourds themselves are not, standing as hefty green sentinels in the autumn fields. Different gourd varieties will have distinctive coloration, ranging from very pale to dark green, sometimes mottled with stripes and spots of white. The gourds are also very heavy, composed at this time of almost 95 percent water. Gourd literature warns the artist to wait patiently for the shell to dry out completely before beginning the creative transformation.

*Carving lightly on a green gourd, like this one
(opposite page), can create unusual results.*

Actually, many things can be done with a green gourd. The green color, contained in the outer epidermal layer of waxy coating, begins to mold as the water evaporates from the shell's interior. The mold creates the lovely mottled effect on the dried gourd's surface. Although artists find inspiration in the mold patterns, sometimes they prefer a completely clear shell. If you remove the outer waxy surface soon after harvesting and wipe moisture from the drying gourd on a regular basis with a light bleach and water solution, the gourd shell will become pale to almost white and completely clear of blemishes or mottled coloring.

Choose mature green gourds free of blemishes.

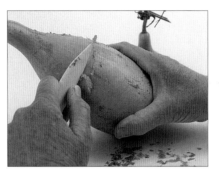

While the gourd is green, use a dull table knife to scrape off the shell's waxy outer layer. A bone folder (scoring tool) or letter opener also works; avoid tools with serrated edges.

After removing the waxy layer, use a kitchen scrubber and warm water to remove remaining bits on the shell. Smooth away any knife marks.

As the gourd dries, wipe away moisture that collects on the gourd's surface. Use a very dilute rinse of antibacterial cleansing solution to make sure the surface remains free of mold.

By carefully using tools designed for making silk screens (film cutters) or linoleum block cuts, you can remove portions of the epidermal layer and then either dye or stain the gourd, using the remaining waxy coating much as a resist. After the gourd is completely dry, the outer skin can be thoroughly cleaned, but the design will remain in the shell. Occasionally, gourds will dry without losing the epidermal layer. The epidermis turns a waxy white or appears as a pale coating on the gourd surface instead of molding and flaking away; it also provides a great contrast to the exposed gourd shell underneath.

With a small blade, Ginger Summit scraped a design into the waxy exterior green surface of this tree gourd, collected soon after it fell. As the green gourd dried, the shell became dark against the lighter scraped pattern. Mayan hieroglyphs inspired the design.

Japanese and Peruvian gourd farmers cut and clean the gourd's interior as well as the outer epidermis immediately after harvesting. This allows the gourd to dry extremely quickly. One drawback is that the edge of the gourd sometimes collapses inward as it dries. If you fill the gourd with silica gel, borax, or materials commonly used to dry flowers, the silica gel or other substance will quickly absorb moisture in the shell. This may help eliminate the threat of withering around the cut surface. Shallow cuts or patterns made in the external shell after harvesting will dry with sometimes unanticipated results. The edges of the cuts shrink slightly and may discolor as the shell continues to dry. However, it's possible to use these lines as the basis for further embellishment when the gourd is completely dry.

A challenge to working with green gourds is that the finished product cannot be predicted. But then, that's part of the adventure and may lead to fascinating results.

Karen Cheeseman

Karen Cheeseman describes her work: "For five years my husband has been growing all the gourds I use on our farm in midwestern Ontario. I wash the green gourds and give them a rinse of ten parts water to one part bleach. Then I carve them using various cutters, including a scalpel, high-speed rotary carver with the flexible shaft, and air-turbine carver. They are then allowed to dry. Unique shapes are created in the drying process, depending on how much water is in them and how fast they dry. I'm never really sure how a gourd will dry (or rot). I really like the unpredictability of this particular process. I used a scalpel knife and peeled off the epidermal layer of the works I call Triangles and Horizontal Bands. When they were dry, I used colored waxes on the gourds, and sealed them with three or four coats of paste floor wax. I'm continuing to experiment with green gourd carving."

In Thailand, fresh vegetable and fruit carving is an ancient popular tradition. Dining tables are graced with elegantly carved fruits and vegetables that create edible bouquets. Noi Thomas, a Thai-American, uses a small sharp carving knife to carve green gourds from her California garden. These deep cuts mean that gourds do not dry hard and rot if not eaten.

Horizontal Bands, Karen Cheeseman

By removing negative space, fretwork creates airy, three-dimensional designs.

FRETWORK
Cutout Designs

*S*ome people may not consider fretwork, or cutout designs, carving, but it is one of many popular methods for decorating and embellishing gourds. In fretwork, the artist cuts with a saw or blade completely through the shell, rather than carving a design on the surface.

In one fretwork style, the artist applies the principal design or pattern to the shell's exterior with woodburning or painting and cuts away the shell surrounding that design. The artist then files and sands the edges, or leaves them as a straight edge with the background removed. For example, the cut for the gourd opening may conform to the design around the gourd's neck.

The artist can cut to use the gourd's interior cavity to contrast with the design by removing negative spaces that surround the design. The depth itself may create a dramatic contrast that could be enhanced if he sprays or colors the interior a bold color. Rocks, shells, or leaves placed inside the gourd could provide still more dimension to the work.

Design motifs or complex scenes that encircle a gourd take advantage of the intrinsic shape of the shell to create more three-dimensional images. When the artist removes all negative space, the shapes on the opposite side of the gourd interact with the visible motif to create greater depth and movement than simple surface embellishment could.

Negative spaces removed from carved gourds can also form a lattice or fretwork in which the openings themselves create the pattern. Position a candle or light inside the hollowed-out gourd to highlight these patterns.

USING HAND TOOLS

Mexican Luminary

If you're new to gourd carving, here is a good place to begin. This Mexican luminary project provides a simple introduction to cutting gourd shells with hand tools to create a decorative table or garden luminary. Ceramic bowls made in Mexico for protecting candles on patio tables inspired the design. Make several with different designs and finishes to help you get comfortable with the variety of tools available for carving gourds. Select small gourds with a round bulb that sit flat on the base. The shell should be dense but not thick.

Mexican Luminary, Ginger Summit

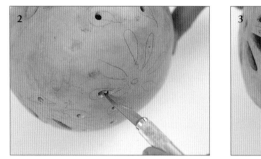

Cut and clean the gourd. Then draw the design on the shell and drill a hole into each portion you want to remove.

Using a saw blade attachment to the hobby knife, cut along the lines of the pattern. After all parts have been removed, use the concave carving blade of the knife to smooth out the cut lines, slanting the edge slightly toward the inside of the gourd. Depending on the design, you may want to drill extra holes for accent openings.

Spray the interior of the gourd black with urethane finish, taking care to wipe off any stray drips immediately. Then sand the exterior and paint or stain. Finish with spray urethane. A ring of Earthquake wax or children's clay will hold the candle securely in the bottom of the luminary.

Make several luminaries, and experiment with different finishes that go with your décor. Finished with nonglossy or matte varnish, the black luminary resembles Mexican pottery. To create a metallic gold finish, try a light rub of gold shoe polish.

USING A POWER JIGSAW

Ginger Summit

Potpourri

This small round gourd is just the right size to hold potpourri leaves and cuttings.

Potpourri, Ginger Summit

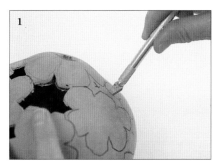

Draw the design on the shell. Then use a hobby knife to make a small cut so that you can insert the power saw blade in the center of the spaces to be removed.

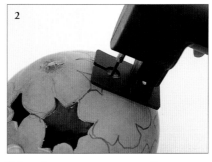

Using the power saw, cut to all corners and remove the negative space. Continue doing this for each section you want to remove. Cut into the angle from each side of the space. Then cut around the gourd's waist to separate top and bottom.

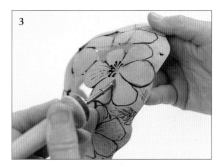

Use a Hot Tool to burn the outlines of leaves and flowers. Make finer lines within each flower with a detail wood-burning tool. If you wish, you can burn the design before cutting out the spaces. Here the artist darkens all petal edges with a wood-burner.

Use a riffler rasp, file, or sandpaper to taper the cut edges around the flowers, making the petals appear more delicate. Sand the interior of the gourd.

Use dyes, inks, or paints to color the design. Don't worry about going over the lines since the background spaces will be carved away. Use a ball-tip rotary carver to lightly texture the background and to remove excess paint.

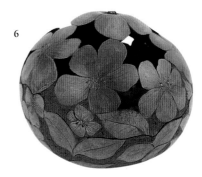

Finish the gourd with spray urethane.

WOOD-BURNER AS CARVING TOOL

Jill Walker

Candle Shield

A snake gourd can be used to make several candle shields, each with a distinctive petroglyph design.

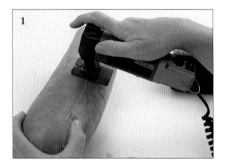

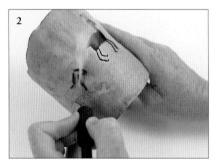

First make an incision and use the saw to make a straight cut around one end of the gourd. Allow about 4 to 6 inches and cut an irregular scalloped edge for the top of the shield.

Clean the interior shell and draw petroglyph designs around the gourd's outer surface.

Using the Razertip wood-burning tool, cut out large design elements. Carefully adjust the heat; the thin snake gourd may burn if the tool is too hot. Keep a damp sponge handy to put out accidental sparks.

After removing large elements, burn the antlers and legs and other linear parts at a cooler temperature. Lightly burn other features. Use the side of the tip to darken the gourd's edges.

Spray the gourd's interior black and protect the exterior surface with a light coat of polyurethane. Put the gourd over a votive candle in a glass holder.

ROTARY-DRILL CARVING TOOL

Cutout Ornaments

Lightweight ornamental gourds can be used to make a wide variety of ornaments to hang on a tree or nestle inside a basket. For a cutout design of spring flowers, first draw a simple flower and leaf outline on a clean, egg-shaped ornamental gourd.

Use a sharp cylinder tip to make a hole in a large area you want to remove. Slowly move the burr along drawn lines. Use a firm grasp and slow movement to cut a smooth line.

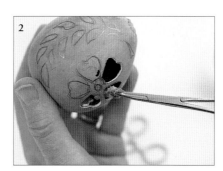

After making a few large openings, use a hemostat (long-handled tweezers) to remove pulp. If you wait until you finish the design, you risk breaking more delicate parts.

When you've removed the pulp, continue to carve the rest. Use a concave blade to smooth edges and remove flakes of inner lining.

Color the ornaments with acrylic paints, stains, or dyes. Drill a small hole at the top of the gourd to glue a bead and hanger made of waxed linen or pearl cotton.

Artist Lillian Hopkins created this tree spirit. The elaborate cutting following the gnarled textures on the bulb of this short-handled dipper gourd creates the perfect root system.

In Autumn Leaves, by artist Mary Segreto, the elaborate cut of the neck complements the delicate contours of the leaf pattern.

Latana Jan Bernier

"My personal mission," Latana Jan Bernier says, "is to maintain my gourds as vessels, a use that dates from early humans. I have chosen not to add wood, clay, or other gourds to force my gourd to become something else.

"Surf and Turf is an exception to this. Although the fish glued onto the gourd is the piece that I cut out to form the basket opening, I didn't have this plan in mind when I began the cut. Generally, large cuts made on a curve stay stuck in the gourd and have to be cut into smaller pieces. Imagine my surprise when the fish just swam out! So the idea to attach it to the gourd was obviously the gourd's idea, not mine."

For Twist and Shout: Horses, Latana Jan Bernier used a charcoal stick to rough in the design elements, keeping a keen eye for balance and interplay between the design and the gourd's shapes. For this

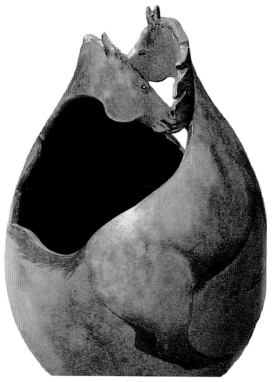

Twist and Shout: Horses

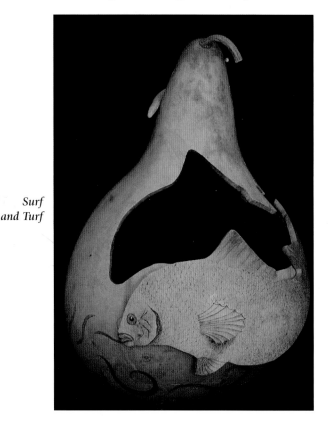

Surf and Turf

gourd, the position of each horse must be such that the horse neck bends realistically along the same curvature as the gourd neck, allowing that wonderful feeling of motion.

"For all my gourds the same task exists—finding the balance between the design and the shape of the gourd so that the design becomes an integral part of the surface," Bernier says.

"At times, the interior is used just as a rough contrast, although on some gourds the interior carving, pyrography, and painting are wonderful elements to complement the outside. I try to keep the interior colors less intense so that the eye focuses on the exterior surface. For colors, my primary coloring agent is Baroque Art Guilders paste, which allows a range of shades from very transparent to intense opaque colors and still allows the gourd's mold stains to show through."

Spawning Salmon, Jeanne Chapman

Jeanne Chapman

By stacking two or more carved gourds together, Jeanne Chapman creates a more three-dimensional look to her containers.

The gourd, Spawning Salmon, was wood-burned with the Hot Tool, colored with leather dyes, and cut out with the MicroLux hobby jigsaw. The bottom piece depicts a raging whitewater river, colored with leather dyes and acrylic paints. A round 25-inch diameter terrarium bowl was planted with a northern woods scene.

Marcia Sairanen

"After choosing a gourd, I draw the design with a soft lead pencil or soapstone pencil. I then use a Detail Master #5A wood-burning pen to burn in the entire design," Marcia Sairanen says. "If I want shading, I use a shading tip. Sometimes I use the different tips with a Walnut Hollow wood-burning pen or the Hot Tool."

Sairanen continues, "To cut a lid or to cut lattice-work on a gourd, I use the MiniCraft hobby jigsaw. For thinner gourds and more elaborate cuts, I use the MicroLux jigsaw. To start the cut for a lid, I use a craft knife to make a narrow slit; then I slip in the fine-tooth saw blade. For lattice cutting, I begin the cut by first drilling a small hole to insert the saw blade. Before staining the gourd with leather dyes, markers, or paste waxes, I make sure all pencil marks are removed. I simply wipe the gourd with a wet paper towel or with cotton soaked in alcohol. This also removes any burning residue. Depending on what coloring I used on the gourd, I finish with a UV-protecting spray or use wax to protect the design."

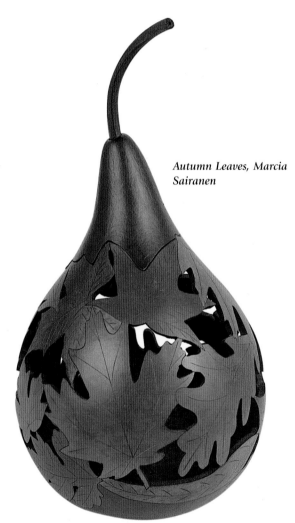

Autumn Leaves, Marcia Sairanen

Jeanne Lee Ames

"My Pacific Northwest Frogs gourd was inspired by a trip to Vancouver Island. First I sketched the design with a pencil and cut it out with a MicroLux jigsaw. Then I wood-burned the design and painted it with acrylics. After everything was dry, I finished it with a polyacrylic finish and painted the inside with gesso."

Pacific Northwest Frogs, Jeanne Lee Ames

Cass Iverson

Cass Iverson carved a canteen gourd into a circle of palm trees and mounted it on a base that holds a glass-enclosed votive candle.

Palm Island, Cass Iverson

Cam Merkle

Cam Merkle made cutouts with a hobby jigsaw and carved all the detailing on the feathers with a Razer-tip wood-burning tool.

Feathers, Cam Merkle

Jack Thorp

"Using a graphite pencil, I first do the initial design layout. Then," Jack Thorp continues, "I cut the gourd using a micro-mini jigsaw. As soon as I complete all the cuts, I file the edges of the cutouts using mini-wood files of various shapes. Before applying any finish on the surface, I sand the gourd lightly with 200-grit fine sandpaper and apply acrylic paint or leather dye with a sea sponge. Finally, I finish the gourd with clear satin-spray sealer."

Spiral-Cut Ball

Blue Fretwork Design

Judy Arrigotti

"I choose large gourds that have thick shells because my carved designs often have intricate shapes and cutouts," Judy Arrigotti says. "As a former art teacher, I have had lots of experience drawing and sketching in other media, so all my designs on gourds are done with pencil, freehand. With experience, I have learned how to create a design that will work effectively without being too fragile. I try not to leave any dangling elements at risk of being chipped or broken off. I also keep in mind how the gourd will be held or carried and not have fragile design elements in the way. After sketching the designs, I wood-burn using a standard chisel tip on the Hot Tool.

"To begin the cutouts, I drill holes in the corners of all portions to be removed. Using a MiniCraft hobby jigsaw, I cut out the designs starting with the smallest sections. The larger portions help support the more fragile parts of the design during this process. I cut out the angles first and then remove the remainder of that section. I remove the small sections all around the gourd before starting on the larger pieces. If I completely carve out one side of the gourd, it will be very fragile while I work in another area. In all of my gourds, there is at least one hole large enough for my hand so that I can clean out the interior of the gourd after it is carved. I remove all the pulp and softer portions of the interior but do not try to sand or smooth the interior surface. I like the textural contrast of the rough inner surface with the finely finished exterior. Sometimes I use paint spray or stain on the interior, but usually I leave it natural.

"Then I paint the carved and burned design, using acrylic paints. When the paint is completely dry, I protect the gourd with a sprayed urethane finish."

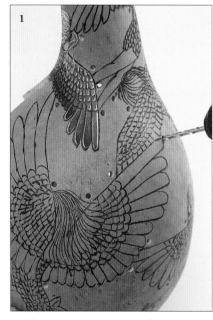

Drill a hole in the corners of all spaces to be removed.

Use a saw to cut out all of the smallest spaces.

Remove the smallest spaces first. The larger background areas provide strength for the overall gourd as you carve.

Completed gourd, Bluebird Girls.

Mast Confusion

Playtime

Family Pride

Whitney Johnson Peckman

"My gourds are all created using a Detail Master, a Dremel rotary carver, and a motley assortment of hand tools, hobby knives, small files, little sanding drums, and the humble emery board. As for technique," Whitney Johnson Peckman says, "I draw everything from my mind, then engrave the lines by burning. Next I do all the painting and engrave again using a small grinding bit to add fine detail. After that is complete, I cut all the spaces using a small spiral or multiuse drill bit (similar to a Rotozip bit). I save the cutting until last so that I can better determine what negative space should come out, not wanting to look through one hole and directly out another. It is important that what is seen through the cutouts is a suggestion of something, so that the viewer is teased into turning the piece. The work is usually different in shading on the back. That means, for example, that one side may appear sunny and the other side shady."

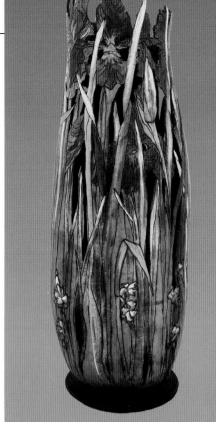

In the Iris Garden, Whitney Johnson Peckman

Dragons in the Poppies, Whitney Johnson Peckman

Ann Mitchell

Indian traditions of Baja, Mexico, inspired Baja Feather Cutouts. Ann Mitchell used the MicroLux high-speed drill for relief carving and the MicroLux cross saw for feather cutouts.

Baja Feather Cutouts, Ann Mitchell

Howard Swerdloff

Howard Swerdloff is a woodworker and sculptor who has spent much of his career designing cabinetry and furniture. Swerdloff recently brought his experience and sense of adventure to gourd carving. He favors large thick-shelled gourds to create lamps, containers, and vases, usually with elaborate scrollwork and carved surfaces. Most of the larger pieces are mounted on a separate gourd stand that complements the cutout designs and shapes. After he creates the basic form, he gives the entire gourd an undercoat inside and out. He then stipples it with multiple stains, paints, and dyes. As a finishing detail, he adds glass beads and painted pods.

Around Adventure. Round fretwork bowl with top.

Fretwork Fancies

FRETWORK SPIRALS

Robert Dillard

Robert Dillard's spiral-cut designs all have a definite number of bands wrapped around each gourd. The width of the spiral cut and the space between each cut is constant from the top to the bottom of each gourd. Of course, the hard part is figuring out how the bands will fit. Measure the circumference of the smallest circle by using a horizontal plane through the gourd (see drawing). Make your first vertical spiral cut at this smallest circle.

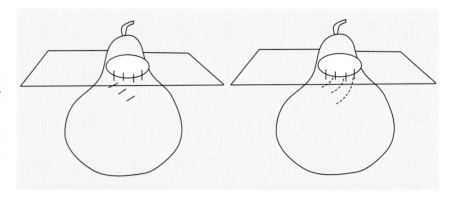

Pass a horizontal plane through the smallest circle of the gourd. Mark your first vertical and diagonal lines (left); then create spiral cuts (right).

"To strengthen the gourd, put braces at various points. These can take on designs of their own, but my preference is to follow a pattern where these braces form spirals down the gourd that are opposite in direction of the original spirals," Dillard says.

"Mark the spirals and braces with graphite pencil, and then spray the gourd with an acetate spray, such as Deft. This is easily removed, along with the pencil marks, later.

"The basic cutting tool I use is the MicroLux mini-jigsaw. First drill a hole with a small bit in the area to be cut and then saw close to but not on the marked lines. Then, depending on the gourd's size and thickness, finish shaping the opening with a hobby knife. Sand; a nail file or an emery board can be useful.

"When all the openings have been made, I clean the inside of the gourd. You can sand the inside, using forceps with sandpaper wrapped around the tips. The interior can be painted, stained, or dyed. Because the exterior is protected with acetate, the interior coloration will not bleed onto the exterior shell. Remove the acetate covering and any pencil marks with #0000 steel wool. Finish the exterior of the gourd, and then protect with a final spray of acetate coating."

Spiral Pear

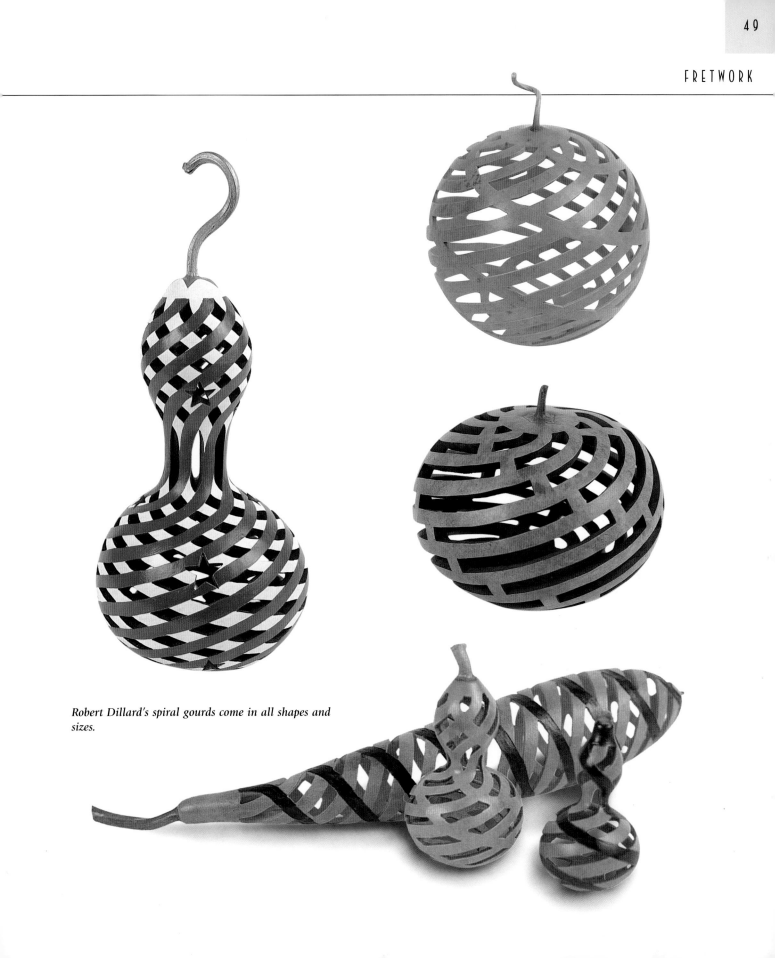

Robert Dillard's spiral gourds come in all shapes and sizes.

Shawn Taylor

"I usually begin by cleaning the gourd with soapy water and then sanding it with fine sandpaper," Shawn Taylor explains. "For my taste, coarse sandpaper removes too much of the natural pattern in the gourd's surface. Then I lay out the design with pencil. My primary tool is the Strong 90 micromotor, a rotary tool. Typically, I first make a large enough hole somewhere in the piece to allow removal of the inner material. It is essential to wear a good painter's mask to keep the gourd particles out of your lungs.

"The next step, critical to creating appealing cutwork, is to bevel the sides of the cuts inward with a hand carving knife. I use the curved hobby carving blades for this purpose. The beveling removes the frayed look that sometimes is created after the initial carving. If space permits, I may attempt to put a flex shaft on the high-speed rotary carving tool and use a Kutzall burr to remove the inside layer of gourd walls. Finally, I straighten the lines, smooth the curves, and sharpen angles with small files.

"I always use leather dyes, even if I am going for a natural look. Occasionally, I will add acrylic paints or Baroque Art Guilders paste. Other embellishments I use include inlaid stones, beads, and feathers."

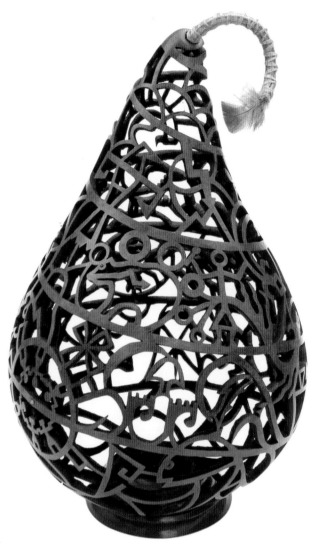

Connections

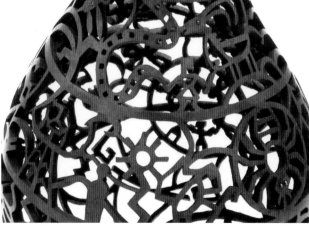

Connections detail.

Snake, Shawn Taylor

Marshall Wiseman

For Fretwork Leaves, his first gourd project, Wiseman used a #15 saw blade in the #2 hobby knife to patiently carve the entire gourd.

Fretwork Leaves,
Marshall Wiseman

Red Lady, Shawn Taylor

The engraver barely cuts or pierces the gourd's surface and removes very little shell.

ENGRAVING

$\mathcal{F}$rom ancient times, gourds embellished with engraved designs have been found on all continents except Antarctica. Many ancient gourds from China, South America, and Africa are works of art that contain such detail and artistic expertise that it's hard to imagine how these treasures were created.

Engraved designs often reveal significant information about the cultures in which they were made, such as details of everyday life, suggestions of rituals or important ceremonies, or homage to supernatural powers. The artists who created these pieces were highly skilled, and even though they were from such different cultures and eras, their tools and techniques were remarkably similar.

Unlike other styles of gourd carving, with engraving the gourd surface is just pierced or cut, and very little of the shell is actually removed. Chinese artists use an engraving needle to scratch a design into the exterior shell; then they carefully apply ink to the inscribed lines.

Artists in South America and Africa use a sharpened nail, called a burin, or another sharpened metal point to incise the shell. Typically, the artist barely pierces the gourd's outer shell, and the line is almost imperceptible to anyone but the artist. After he completes the design, oil and soot are massaged into the shell, carefully filling in all the carved lines. After he wipes away the paste, the lines of the design stand out black against the shell. He then washes the gourd to remove any residue left on the shell.

Although the subject matter might have been adapted to reflect changes in daily life, the tools and techniques have barely changed over the centuries. Engraved gourds continue to be created in much the same traditional ways in many parts of the world today.

Chinese needle-engraved gourd. Collection of Norma A. Fox.

SCRIMSHAW ENGRAVING

Gertrude Turner

Scrimshaw is a carving technique most often associated with designs on ivory and whalebone created by sailors using images from their adventures at sea. The process follows the same steps as other engraving methods, but here the artist uses a scalpel. After the artist polishes the surface so that it's smooth, she cuts the design with a sharp blade and then darkens it with soot or inks.

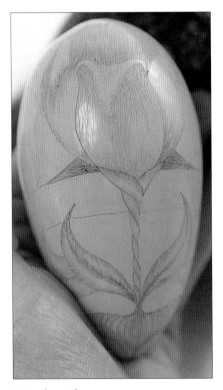

Scrimshaw Flower

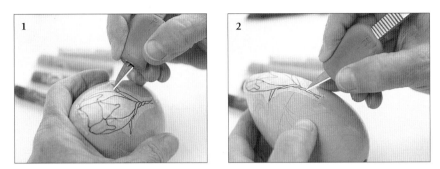

Draw the design on tissue paper adhered to the prepared surface of an egg-shaped gourd. Use a sharp blade to cut through the paper into the gourd shell. The paper provides a guide and strengthens the shell so that it doesn't chip.

After cutting main outlines, remove the paper and cut straight hatch marks to provide depth and shading.

After finishing the engraving, use oil pastels to color the design.

With your finger, push pigment into the engraved cuts and use cheesecloth to wipe off excess, leaving color only in the engraved cuts. Then rub beeswax into the surface to protect the pigments.

As soon as all colors are rubbed into the design, polish the gourd with a soft cloth.

ENGRAVING USING A BURIN

Tito Medina

Tito Medina uses his Peruvian burin, which he resharpens to create a very fine-line design inspired by Chinese needle-engraved gourds.

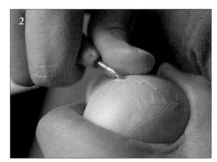

Holding the egg gourd firmly with one hand, Medina pushes the burin just enough to scratch through the exterior surface of the shell, making a baseline around the gourd.

The same tool is used to make all the lines in the design.

The finished design.

Medina rubs the soot paste into the design and wipes the excess off the outer shell.

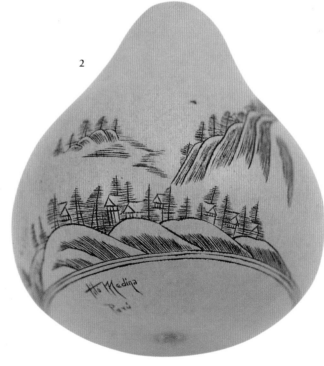

Hills and Houses, the finished gourd by Tito Medina, was inspired by Chinese needle-engraved gourds.

ENGRAVING USING POWER TOOLS

Ginger Summit

Many burrs are designed specifically for engraving with rotary carvers. Those with the diamond tip are particularly effective for making very fine lines suitable for etching and engraving projects. It is important to use the flexible-shaft attachment because handheld models are often too heavy to guide in creating fine lines. Carvers powered by air are ideal for this technique because both the fine tips and the rapid rotation speed allow for effortless detailed carving.

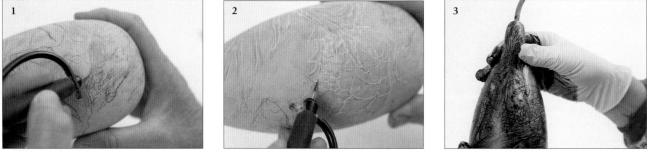

Using a pencil, Summit first drew the design freehand on the gourd. "Because a small mottled section at the base of the gourd resembled a bumpy head, a dragon immediately seemed to drape its body and wings around the gourd," Summit thought. Using a Turbocarver and an engraving bit, she carved the outline, then added shading and details with the finest bits.

Wearing rubber gloves, Summit thoroughly massaged the gourd, making sure that the paste was in every carved line.

SAFETY NOTE

Although tempting, do not use photocopier toner for the paste. Photocopier toner is very toxic if inhaled. The particles are so fine that they will easily pass through most filtering systems, and being plastic, instead of breaking down, they will react with lung tissue. It's not worth the risk.

ENGRAVED GOURDS BY GINGER SUMMIT

Sail Away Home. Scrimshaw and etchings of old sailing vessels inspired the designs on this gourd. It was carved using the Turbocarver with several different tips to provide some contrast between ships, sails, and water.

Summer Bouquet. This bottle gourd was designed with buds on the gourd's small upper portion and flowers in full bloom around the lower portion. It was engraved with the Turbocarver.

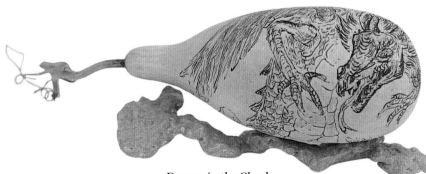

Dragon in the Clouds

Miniature Rose. While growing, this small gourd was shaped between two boards by Jim Story. It was green-scraped, which left a very pale surface. The roses were engraved with the Turbocarver and a diamond engraving tip.

This ancient Peruvian gourd reveals the visible, scorched detail of the Staff God.
Courtesy of the Phoebe Apperson Hearst Museum of Anthropology and the Regents of the University of California, Berkeley.

Tito Medina, using ancient carving and scorching techniques, recreates the Peruvian image using the previous photo and a detailed drawing made by Lawrence Dawson at the anthropology museum.

Here is Tito Medina's reproduction of the Peruvian gourd (far left) thought to be over 2,000 years old.

Julio Seguil Ríos

Before engraving or carving a gourd, Julio Seguil Ríos sharpens the burin and cutting blade on a sharpening stone.

First the artist carves the gourd with a burin.

Next he burns a bundle of ichu, a native grass, then mixes it with salad oil to create a thick soot paste. (You can also burn newspapers to get the desired carbon soot.)

He puts soot in the palm of the hand.

He mixes the soot with vegetable oil to make a paste.

Ríos rubs the carved gourd to get the pigments into all the carved lines.

Here is the blackened gourd.

The artist rinses the gourd in water to remove excess soot.

Intricate details of jungle life.

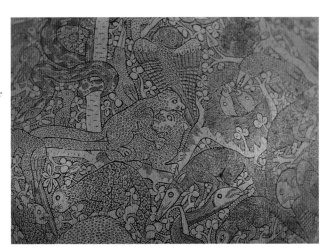

Large carved gourd showing scenes of village life.

This gourd was carved and burned to create a variety of textures and shading to show scenes of village life.

DYED FIRST, THEN ENGRAVED

Tito Medina

These gourds were dyed by boiling them in fabric dyes found in Peruvian markets.

Medina carves the dyed gourd with a burin, revealing the pale inner shell.

TITO MEDINA'S SCENES FROM PERU

Finished gourds, showing the light carved design in contrast to the brightly dyed shell.

ENGRAVED, THEN SCORCHED OR BLACKENED

Village Scene, engraved and scorched.

Musicians, engraved and scorched.

Tito Medina engraved Dancers with a burin and blackened the design with soot and oil.

Dyeing or painting the gourd before or after linear carving will produce different effects.

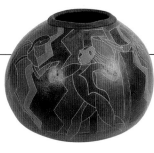

LINEAR CARVING

$\mathcal{W}$hat we've called linear carving is often similar to engraving techniques. The artist creates the design by drawing with a carving tool on the gourd shell. With engraving, lines are finely cut or scratched, and little if any of the shell is actually removed. When more of the shell is removed, a different effect is created.

Both hand and power tools can be used for this carving style. Appropriate hand tools are the narrow gouges, such as 2-mm veiners (U-shape) or #9 gouges or V-shapers. (For an explanation of these numbers, see Carving with Gouges, p. 89.) In general, the curved U-shape is easier to control than the "V" on a hard gourd shell.

In addition to these tools, gourd artists in many parts of the world prefer blades and traditional carving tools that have been used in their culture for centuries. The traditional techniques appear simple but have in fact taken years to master.

More recently, power tools have provided an easy option for gourd artists. With the wide variety of tools, accessories, and burrs (or carving tips) available, carving designs on gourds has become a fast and adaptable decorative technique, used either by itself or combined with other embellishment methods, such as pyrography, painting, and inlay.

One variable of this carving technique is the different effects that can be created by varying the sequence of carving with steps such as dyeing or painting. If the gourd shell is colored first (with either dyes or paints) and then carved, the relatively pale carved-out portions will stand in dramatic contrast to the darker surface. When the gourd is carved first and then dyed, the soft inner shell exposed by the carving will absorb more of the color and appear much darker than the surface exterior shell. If painted with opaque paint, such as acrylics, the carved lines will simply appear as a depression in the surface of the gourd. Often artists will use a combination of these techniques on the same gourd.

CULTURAL EXAMPLES OF LINEAR CARVING

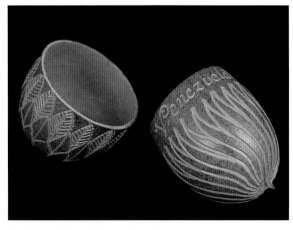

Pod from Venezuela.   Collection of Poco-a-Poco.

Chinese gourd.   Collection of the author.

Korean bowl.   Collection of Carol Morrison.

Korea

The main portions of the design on this Korean gourd bowl were carved and then stained to create the visible dark outlines. Then portions of the loom and bench were carved away, revealing the lighter inner gourd shell, creating contrast and depth within the design.

China

This Chinese gourd was first dyed, and then calligraphy was painted on the surface. The black calligraphy was then outlined with carving to help separate it from the background. Additional writing was added by carving into the upper bulb.

Guatemala

In Central and South America, many so-called gourds are really tree gourds, or pods from the *Crescentia cujete* (calabash tree) and *Crescentia alata* (or *Parmentiera alata*) trees. These trees are also known as *morro* or *jícara*. From the *C. alata* tree come the small spherical containers known as *guacol* or *huacal*, which are used as bowls or water containers. The *C. cujete* tree produces ellipsoidal fruits, called jícara or huacal, which are commonly cut in half and used as utensils. These gourds may be left plain, but when decorated, they become highly prized items. Containers made from fruits of the *Cucurbit* vines, called calabaza, are generally not nearly as popular as the tree gourds. They are seldom decorated, but if embellished, they are usually painted.

The Guatemalan town of Rabinal is well known for its special technique of gourd engraving, sometimes called black-and-white carving. First the artist thoroughly cleans the epidermal skin from a green gourd, the fruit of the morro or jícara tree. He then dries the gourd in the sun and rubs it with the abrasive leaves of an evergreen oak tree to remove any blemishes.

After he dries and polishes the gourd, he covers it with a lacquer called *nij*. This lacquer is made from the insect *Cocus nige*, which is boiled and then ground into a waxy paste. Any discoloration is removed by dissolving it in alcohol, which creates a clear wax. This lacquer is then mixed with linseed oil and rubbed on the gourd until a high gloss is achieved.

After this process, he next dyes the shiny lacquered gourd with lampblack, obtained from the ash of pitch-pine mixed with grease. After all these preparatory steps, the gourd is finally ready to be carved with a burin or another chisel type of blade.

Photos and discussion of Guatemalan gourds courtesy of Kathy Rousso in Rabinal, Baja Vera Paz, Guatemala, in 2002 with Fulbright funding.

These gourds, or morros, were freshly harvested. Photo by Kathy Rousso.

These gourds are being soaked and boiled in water to clean out the insides.
Photo by Kathy Rousso.

Nij is made from bugs similar to cochineal bugs. The bugs are spread out on tree branches and left for a year, where they grow and multiply, and then are collected and boiled. Nij makes a natural lacquer.
Photo by Kathy Rousso.

An artist rubs nij on the gourd.
Photo by Kathy Rousso.

She rubs the ocote ash onto the lacquered gourd over the nij, while the lacquer is still tacky. This gives the gourd a lustrous shine. Photo by Kathy Rousso.

Finally she carves the pattern.
Photo by Kathy Rousso.

This traditional carved gourd is from Rabinal, Guatemala.
Photo by Kathy Rousso.

The Rabinal, Guatemala, Sunday market. Photo by Kathy Rousso.

USING POWER TOOLS FOR LINEAR CARVING

For several small bowls, Ginger Summit chose a design of interlocking spirals, found in ancient carvings and paintings.

Here's an easy way to divide the gourd's surface into equal sections. Cut a piece of adding-machine paper to fit around the gourd's circumference.

Remove the paper and fold it into halves, fourths, or fifths, whatever division fits the design on the gourd shell. Replace the paper around the gourd. Because four spirals fit this particular gourd, she folded the paper into fourths and made corresponding marks on the gourd to divide it into even quarters.

Use a pencil to draw the design on the gourd.

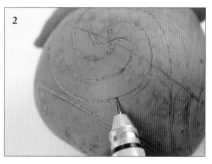

Trace the pencil lines, using a rotary hand-carving tool with a fine ball-tip burr. This makes the design visible after the gourd shell has been dyed or painted.

Wash off the pencil lines and use fine sandpaper to lightly sand the gourd's surface.

Dye the gourd shell. For this gourd, she used Fiebings cordovan dye.

Follow lines previously carved with the fine burr, and carve the pattern lines again with a thicker ball-tip burr.

The lighter surface of the inner shell sharply contrasts with the darker dyed epidermis.

These gourds illustrate the different effects you can achieve by simple variations on this technique.

After the spirals were carved, the gourd was dyed black. When the dye was dry, the carved lines were filled in with white grout. After the grout was thoroughly dry, the gourd was lightly sanded and finished with spray urethane.

First the design on this gourd was carved, and then the entire surface was colored with dye. The softer inner shell absorbed more of the dye and appears darker against the outer gourd surface.

Because this gourd was especially thick, the design swirls were carved much deeper and wider, using a large ball-tip sanding burr. The gourd was sanded with a fine sanding pad, with special care to remove any irregularities in the indentations. After all the carved lines were made even, the entire surface was dyed. Several coats of wax make this gourd very smooth to the touch.

Using the same technique, this thick canteen gourd was carved with the labyrinth design found on the floor of the Chartres Cathedral in France. Similar finger-shaped labyrinths have been used as meditation aids for thousands of years.

Dyan Mai Peterson

Sometimes all that's required to make a piece stand out are a few accent dots carved in the gourd. For the work Expressions 2002, tools used included a handheld rotary carver, using a ³⁄₁₆-inch round ball-tip cutter with a ³⁄₃₂-inch shank.

The gourd Asian Influence was first dyed, and then portions surrounding the body were painted or stained black. It was then carved with the incursion technique. Using a handheld rotary carver, Peterson chose a cylinder square crosscut burr with a ³⁄₃₂-inch shank and ¹⁄₁₆-inch diameter cylinder. Some carved symbols are abstract shapes, and others have specific meanings, such as happiness, harmony, love, friendship, and prosperity.

Expressions 2002, Dyan Mai Peterson

Asian Influence, Dyan Mai Peterson

Cindy Lee

To create Birds Fly on a Cool Breeze, Cindy Lee stained the gourd, carved calligraphy into its surface, and threaded cord through beads secured to the neck of the gourd.

Birds Fly on a Cool Breeze,
Cindy Lee

Pueblo Nights, Rhoda Forbes

Rhoda Forbes

After Rhoda Forbes sponge-painted the gourd Pueblo Nights, she used a high-speed rotary carver and a small engraving bit to draw the design freehand. On top of the gourd she wrapped coiling around a foundation of pine needles.

Forbes advises: "When using a high-speed rotary carver with an engraving bit on a painted piece, clean the bit periodically. Paint will build up on it. This is especially important when the surface, like this one, has many layers of sponged paint."

Eugene Endicott

Eugene Endicott's simple linear carving for Petroglyphs creates a pleasing design.

Petroglyphs, Eugene Endicott

Gwen Heineman

"All my work is inspired by nature," Gwen Heineman says, "After painting or staining the whole gourd surface, I carve the designs freehand with a high-speed rotary carver, using different sizes of ball-tip cutting burrs. By varying the pressure, the same bits are used to carve simple lines thick or thin, gouge deep into the skin, or remove large sections of the surface. The sizes of the ridges, or flutes, on the bits affect the texture of the design. After I finish carving, I paint additional details on. Then I spray on a layer of Krylon acrylic sealer for protection."

Fall Harvest

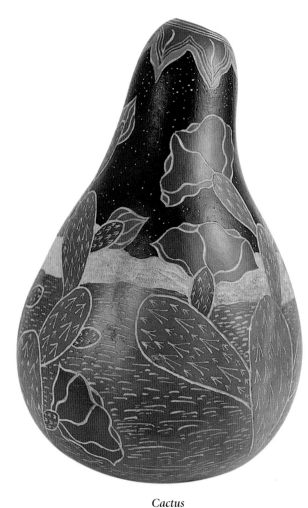

Cactus

Lily Pond

Debra Toth

Gourd artist Debra Toth first draws and dyes the patterns and designs on the gourd shell. Then, with the carving tool, she outlines all sections of the design. The light outlines emphasize the movement and complex interwoven shapes that create these dramatic patterns. Note especially the treatment of the rim on the neck of the gourd. Geometric designs complementing patterns on the body were burned, dyed, or carved to make the rim an integral part of the overall design.

"Currently I am using a variable-speed Dremel with a flexible shaft. I use the 1⁄32-inch or 1⁄16-inch engraving cutters. For color, I favor using dyes from many different manufacturers," Toth says.

Toth's incised gourd Crisp and to the Point was finished with leather dyes, acrylic paint, and wood-burned rim accents. The incised gourd Circle Dancers was made with leather dyes and a leather rim accent. Double Helix Dancers and Family Portraits are incised gourds with leather dyes and wood-burned rim accents. Streets of Gold uses both leather dyes and gold leaf.

Family Portraits

Circle Dancers

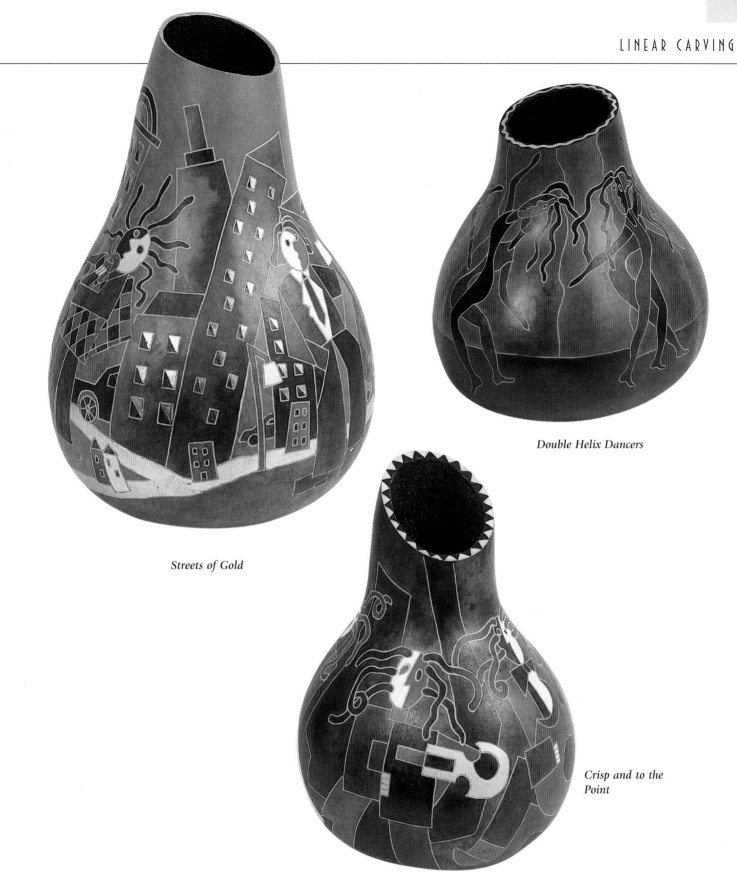

Streets of Gold

Double Helix Dancers

Crisp and to the
Point

Liza Muhly

"I use a Powercrafter pneumatic carving tool with a flexible shaft that can grip a variety of carving tips. Friends have given me some, and I've appropriated many from my dentist," Liza Muhly says. "I first carve part of the design on the gourd and then rub black dye into the lines. I rub this in so that the lines are completely filled. Then I scrub and sand the dye off the surface. I paint the rest of the motif onto the gourd, and when the paint is completely dry, I carve more lines to create the contrast-ing pale lines against the painted background. Finally, I polish and seal the piece with a urethane fin-ish. I am constantly adapting my techniques, to the gourd, the mood, and what I am trying to express."

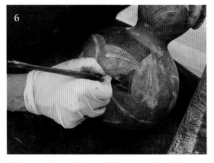

For the artwork Feathers, Liza Muhly draws her design on the gourd, carves lines with a pneumatic drill, and paints the gourd with acrylic paint. When the paint dries, she sands the gourd to remove surface paint, leaving carved lines dark.

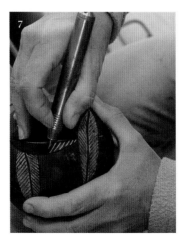

She paints sections of the gourd with leather dye and then carves more details on painted surfaces.

Grasses

Feathers

Water-Lily

Julie Steiner

"In a day of unexpected good luck, I was inspired to use petroglyphs for my designs on gourds," Julie Steiner says. "We were searching for Nevada ghost towns far from where we live. While searching without success for one that seemed near home, we discovered hundreds of petroglyphs all over the rocks, everywhere we looked. Early travelers and the local forest service had documented these simple drawings, and I really liked the primitive approach the original artists took to record their observations on the rocks. My gourds use these petroglyphs along with native poetry.

"I first stain the gourds dark brown, because this provides the best color contrast with the undershell exposed by the carving. As for carving tools, I use a Dremel MultiPro tool with dual speeds, with carbide bits that are either ball-tip cutting heads or cylinders with a rounded head. While working on gourds, I prefer using the lowest speed. That's because vibrations at higher speeds are very hard on my hands and wrist."

Carved Gourd Fragment, Julie Steiner

Blissful Heart, Julie Steiner

*Elephant Mask,
Jerry Lewis*

Jerry Lewis

To create Elephant Mask, Lewis used three different rotary bits: the 3/16-inch cylinder, the 1/4-inch inverted cone, and finally the 5/16-inch cylinder.

GOURD CALLIGRAPHY

Dege Lowry

Dege Lowry uses very small carving tools—gouges, a V-tool, and a battery-operated rotary tool with a ¾-inch and a 5/16-inch cone-shaped burr.

She draws the letters on the gourd with various calligraphic tools, pens, double pencils, or whatever works for her in the space. She does initial carving with the V-tool to outline all details. Background or negative space is carved away with larger gouges. To smooth out any rough surfaces, she finishes with a rotary sanding tool.

Before dyeing the gourd, she wipes the entire gourd with rubbing alcohol to remove any residue or pen marks. For stubborn marks she sometimes uses nail-polish remover. She uses a combination of leather dyes, fabric dyes, and wood stains. If she finds there isn't enough contrast between the design and the background, she uses a small paintbrush with a darker shade to fill in the area.

Lowry's finish is either neutral shoe polish or Krylon clear-coat spray. Sometimes she inlays negative areas with colored sand.

"I like the positive-negative effects that carving creates. The letter bodies generally are positive while their ascenders and descenders become negatives, which create interesting patterns," Lowry says.

*In chip carving, chips or pieces of
gourd shell are removed.*

CHIP CARVING

One gourd-carving style involves removing portions of the shell's outer surface to create a pattern or design. The term *chip carving* is sometimes used to include all such types of carving, no matter what tools, designs, or techniques are used.

Within this very broad definition we include many distinctly different types of carving, such as those done with gouges, and carvings using all shapes and sizes of blades. Chip carving is done all over the world. The unifying element is that chips, or pieces of the shell, are removed during carving to create the design. This distinguishes it from relief carving or figure-ground techniques, which we'll consider in later chapters.

A narrower definition of the term *chip carving* refers to a particular carving style that originated in Europe many centuries ago. Cultural groups throughout this region all used similar tools and techniques to create styles and motifs unique to their areas. Although commonly identified with Switzerland, *chip-carving* traditions flourished throughout eastern European countries and in Scandinavia. In more recent times, these styles have blended. Today chip carving includes a few standard design elements as well as variations that encompass all the traditions. Besides the distinctive design style, the unifying features of chip carving are the shapes of the carving tools and how they are held and used.

Traditional chip carving consists of designs created from combinations of a basic wedge, or triangle, cut. Generally, two knives are employed. One has a short, semicircular blade with the flat cutting edge very close to the handle. It is held in two different positions, depending on the stroke, but always with the grasp of the hand close enough to the blade so that the combined movement of thumb and wrist control the direction and depth of cut. The second knife is called a stab knife and looks much like a skewed-edge chisel. The basic triangles, or wedges, can be assembled in many different combinations to create borders or overall patterns. The triangle can be elongated and even curved to create more elaborate motifs, often within a round or circular pattern.

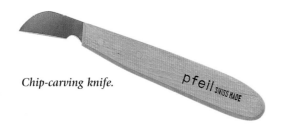

Chip-carving knife.

Traditional chip carving is done on flat softwood, especially basswood. Probably because gourds are neither flat nor soft, gourd carvers have largely neglected this style of carving. However, the simplicity of the designs and tools are intriguing and, with some adaptation, may one day become a popular technique for embellishing gourds.

CHOOSING A GOURD

Because chip carving requires relatively deep incisions into the shell, the gourd must be reasonably thick. Instruction books on chip carving recommend using soft, fresh wood because wood that is older and dry has a tendency to splinter during carving.

Using this advice, select a thick, heavy gourd that is as fresh as possible but still completely dry. (A green gourd carved with this technique would probably

mold and collapse while drying.) Look for a surface completely free of blemishes because blemishes may indicate variable density within the shell. Since the design is in the carved-out patterns, try to find a gourd with uniform coloration. A mottled surface pattern could detract from the main design.

Because the gourd shell is round and harder than the wood traditionally used for chip carving, techniques for holding the knife and the actual carving may have to be adapted.

ADAPTING TRADITIONAL CHIP CARVING TO A GOURD

Ginger Summit

Making a linear border pattern is a good way to practice chip-carving style. Draw two parallel lines about ⅓ inch apart around the rim of a gourd bowl. Then connect the lines to make squares completely around the gourd. Finally, within each square, draw intersecting diagonal lines so that you divide each square into four triangles.

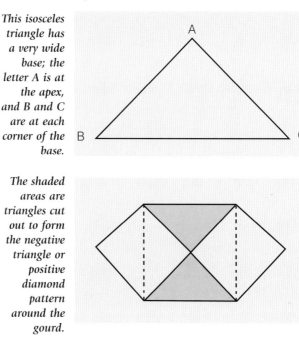

This isosceles triangle has a very wide base; the letter A is at the apex, and B and C are at each corner of the base.

The shaded areas are triangles cut out to form the negative triangle or positive diamond pattern around the gourd.

To make the first pull-cut, hold the knife close to the blade with the sharp edge facing you. Push the knife into triangle point A (see diagram on p. 80) and draw it toward you, pulling the blade out as it reaches the edge of point B. Angle the knife blade toward the triangle's center, not perpendicular to AB.

The second cut is a push-cut. Turn the gourd over and hold the knife so that the sharp edge faces away from you and toward the triangle's center. Push the knife blade into point A of the triangle. Then push it gently up to point C, the other corner of the triangle.

The third cut is another pull-cut. Turn the gourd over again, and again hold the knife with its sharp edge facing you. Slowly push the blade into the triangle's corner B and pull it to the end of the second cut, C. This triangular wedge should pop out. The deepest point of the wedge shape will be in the center of the triangle. Repeat the cuts just a little deeper if the wedge does not pop out.

Finished gourd, Ginger Summit.

The outer shell on this gourd was first completely removed by using a sanding drum on the rotary power carver. This technique is often used in Nigeria. "I wanted to see if removing the more dense outer shell would make the carving easier. It did, indeed, appear to have some effect. After the entire gourd was carved, I dyed it with a leather stain. Rubbing with a fine sanding pad, I lightened the gourd's surface to bring out the contrast with the carved design," Ginger Summit says.

Summit used a knife with a slightly longer blade to carve this design with elongated triangles.

USING THE CHISEL BLADE

Tito Medina

Master carver Tito Medina uses the burin, a sharp engraving tool, to engrave finely detailed scenes that cover the gourd shell. He was introduced to chip carving in a recent trip from his native Peru to the United States.

After trying a few blades in a carving set, he chose the flat #1-sweep, 7-mm chisel to experiment. He grasped the tool in a way similar to that of traditional chip carvers by bracing the thumb against both knife blade and the gourd shell while cutting.

He first drew general outlines on the gourd shell and practiced making small triangular cuts for a bor-der design. With that mastered, he created more elon-gated triangles and other shapes to completely cover the gourd shell. Even though he utilized the tool and design elements of more traditional chip carvers, his designs were original. After Medina returned to Peru, he continued to experiment with the new tools and possibilities of design. The results are an impressive collection of carved gourds, which will challenge every artist.

This entire chip-carving project is done with just the #1, 7-mm flat chisel. Medina's chip carving is not in the traditional Scandinavian style. Instead of cut-ting all the way around the chip before removing it, he cuts and flicks out each partial chip until he has achieved his desired shape.

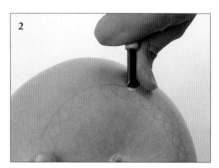

Artist Tito Medina pushes the flat #1, 7-mm chisel at an angle along the line into the gourd.

He flicks the chisel up to remove the chip.

He reinserts the chisel along a line adja-cent to the last cut at an angle into the gourd. He flicks the chisel up to remove the chip.

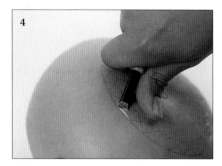

He reinserts the chisel along one of the sides of the triangle. He flicks the chisel up to remove the chip and reinserts the chisel along the line.

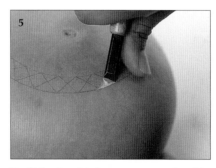

He flicks the chisel up to remove the chip and inserts the chisel on the other side of the triangle.

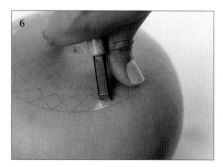

He inserts the chisel at an angle, more deeply at the edge closest to the vertex. He reinserts the chisel further along the line. He flicks the chisel up to remove the chip. He cleans up the edges of the lines.

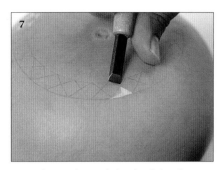

Note the angles and depth of the three cuts.

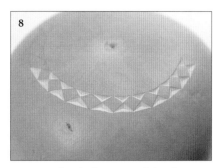

Here is a finished section of the chip-carved bottom of the gourd.

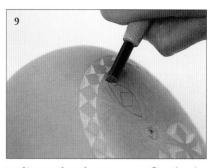

Medina pushes the #1, 7-mm flat chisel at an angle along the line into the gourd. He flicks the chisel up to remove the chip.

He reinserts the chisel along the line adjacent to the last cut at an angle into the gourd. He flicks the chisel up to remove the chip.

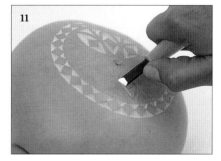

He inserts the chisel into the opposite leg of the triangle. He flicks the chisel up to remove the chip.

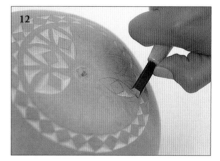

He reinserts the chisel along the line adjacent to the last cut at an angle into the gourd. He flicks the chisel up to remove the chip.

Medina turns the gourd and inserts the chisel into a new face. He flicks the chisel up to remove the chip.

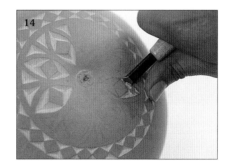

He reinserts the chisel along the line. He flicks the chisel up to remove the chip.

He inserts the chisel along the inside triangular line. He flicks the chisel up to remove the chip.

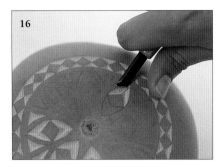

Medina cleans up lines with the chisel and removes excess material.

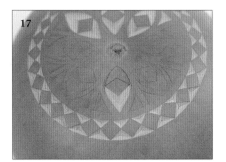

Here is the completed section.

He makes the first insertion.

He inserts the chisel on the second side at an angel.

He inserts the chisel on the third side.

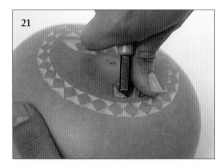

He inserts the chisel adjacent to the first insertion.

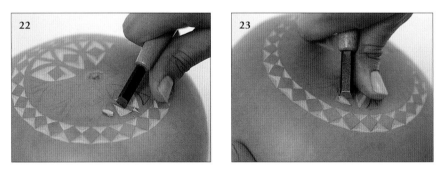

Medina flicks the chisel up to remove the chip and cleans up the cut.

Artist Tito Medina works on the side of the gourd bowl.

He inserts the chisel. He flicks up the chisel to remove the chip.

He cleans up the cut.

Completed side and rim of bowl.

This is a reproduction of a Yoruba gourd bowl motif (see the original container on p. 13).

Medina uses a #3, 8-mm straight gouge to create a design.

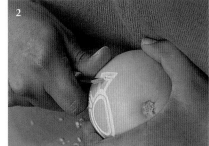

He uses a #1, 7-mm flat chisel at an angle to create one side of the pattern of ridges.

He flips the gourd around 180 degrees and uses a #1, 7-mm flat chisel at an angle to create the opposite side of the ridge pattern.

He continues to cut ridges.

After he completes a set of parallel ridges, Medina turns the gourd 90 degrees and cuts a series of ridges perpendicular to the first set. He holds the skew chisel at an angle on the ridge and pushes down through the set of ridges previously cut.

He pushes the chisel all the way down to the depth desired.

Then Medina turns the gourd 180 degrees and inserts the chisel at an angle beginning at the same line of the previous cut. He moves the chisel along the same line and pushes down again.

He pushes down to the desired depth. He removes the line of chips.

He uses a #1, 7-mm flat chisel at an angle to set apart the center oval in the bird's body.

After making a series of parallel ridges, he makes an angled cut perpendicular to the ridges.

He flips the gourd over 180 degrees and makes the second angled cut along the same ridge.

Here is the finished Yoruba bird motif.

CHIP-CARVED GOURDS BY TITO MEDINA

This carving with ovals and diamonds is based on traditional chip-carving patterns.

Plant Spirals

Sunflower Mountain

Globe Parachute

*Gouges can create
fine lines, dots,
and elongated scoops, or
clear background areas.*

CARVING WITH GOUGES

*T*he gouge is a hand tool that has been used for centuries to carve wood and other relatively soft materials. Blades come in many different shapes and sizes, some of which are particularly useful for the gourd carver. The straightedge tools are usually referred to as chisels, with the sharpened edge either perpendicular or at an angle to the handle. Some carvers use chisels for cleaning out large areas of background around a design as well as for chip carving, as demonstrated by Tito Medina (see p. 98).

Unlike the chisel and chip-carving blades, gouges have blades in various widths that are shaped in a curve, like the truncated bowl of a spoon, or a V-shape, with the cutting edge perpendicular to the handle. The curved gouges are quite popular and versatile for carving gourds. With practice, they can be used to create fine lines, dots, and elongated scoops or to clear out large areas of background around a design. Frequently, artists find that one size or shape is particularly suited to their style of carving. However, the wide range of shapes and sizes can be used to create many different effects. The V-shapes (called V-parting tools) are used primarily for fine lines or specific triangle accents to patterns.

The curve of the gouge tool is described by two numbers: (1) the sweep, or the curvature of the cutting edge, and (2) the width from one corner of the cutting edge to the other, measured in inches or millimeters. Gouge sweeps range from flat (#1) to semicircular (#11). When the sides of the semicircular blades are deeper, forming a U-shape, the gouge is called a veiner. The shank of the gouge can be either straight or spoon-shaped, and it also varies in length.

Variety of gouges.

The gouge handle's shape is an important consideration. Some are longer and designed to be grasped; others are stubby, rounded, and intended to be cradled in the palm. In general, the motion of carving gourds with the gouge is a combination of pushing and twisting or rocking the tool, so the handle's shape is quite important once you develop a preference for a particular carving style or technique. Gouges are available in sets of six or more tools—an excellent way for beginners to experiment with new tools on gourd shells. As you identify favorite shapes of both blades and handles, you can buy individual gouges from specialty wood-carving stores or catalogs.

Some carvers prefer to use a powered gouge carver because it requires less wrist action. The reciprocating action happens only when the gouge touches the work to be carved.

Reciprocating-gouge power tool and safety gloves.

SAMPLER

Ginger Summit

To become familiar with all the different sizes of gouges collected over the years, Ginger Summit explains, "I planned a kind of sampler design that would allow freedom to experiment with the tools and a variety of patterns that could be made with them—wild geese poking through weeds on a gravelly surface."

The outlines of the geese were sketched with a pencil on a smooth gourd shell, and then traced using a #9, 2-mm gouge. By rocking the gouge slightly from side to side while pushing forward, it was quite easy to follow the outlines by moving both the gourd and the gouge at the same time. The outlines were darkened with leather dye to help visualize the overall design. Different sizes of gouges were then used to create a variety of feather patterns on each goose. "Because I wanted to emphasize the feather edges of the cuts, wide gouges were rocked with slightly more motion, creating the roughness of the edges. Small dotted patterns were created with the smallest gouges, pushing straight into the gourd shell and twisting to cut a dot."

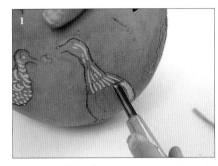

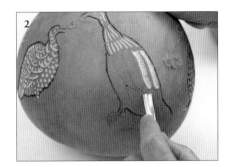

For some of the feather patterns, Summit first made a stop-cut with the gouge by pushing the tool straight down into the surface of the shell where she wanted the cut to end.

Then pulling the tool an inch or more back from the stop-cut, she made the feather cut leading up to the stop-cut. This created a U-shape of overlapping feathers.

Summit created the gravel effect by playing with all the different gouge shapes and sizes and making small cuts and twists at random.

To produce weeds, Summit made fine cuts with the V-parting tool because it gives a much narrower groove than the round gouges.

After the carving was completed, Summit stained the geese with a variety of leather dyes and colored waxes. Excess colors on the shell surface were removed with alcohol. Finally, the gourd was sanded and waxed.

The rim of the gourd was embellished with date palms and various dried pods.

BIRDHOUSES

Marilyn Rehm

Marilyn Rehm and her father, Dr. Leslie Miller, are generally acknowledged to be the artists who introduced carving with gouges to the gourd community. Miller used many different techniques to create unique designs as well as story gourds. (See Dr. Miller's designs on pp. 164–165.) Rehm and her children continue the family tradition of carving using gouges and teaching others.

Only three elements make up this type of geometrical carving: the stop-cut, the chip, and the line. Holding the gouge at a right angle (perpendicular) to the gourd surface and pushing firmly into the gourd shell makes the stop-cut. When the gouge digs in, it makes a thin "U."

"The purpose of the stop-cut," Rehm says, "is to make each chip pop out neat and clean. Moving the gouge back from the stop-cut and lowering the angle of the gouge so it will dig into the gourd makes the chip." She advises using a gentle rocking motion of the wrist when cutting with the gouge. "When it reaches the stop-cut, the cut stops the forward progress of the gouge and the chip falls out. The angle at which the gouge is held determines the depth of carving. It is not necessary to carve deeply. To carve a line, no stop-cut is necessary; just keep pushing the gouge forward."

USING HAND GOUGES

Leah Comerford

Before crafting an open gourd, Leah Comerford says, "I always clean and paint the inside of the gourd so I won't be breathing gourd dust as I work. For this gourd, I planned to work a design of lines carved with the gouge tool around a central area where I'll inset a cabochon." With a small compass, she draws a partial circle around the inlay area.

"Choosing a #9-sweep, ¼-inch gouge, I hold the blade perpendicular to the drawn arc so I can measure the width to the next arc to be drawn. With one side of the blade touching the arc, I put a pencil dot where the other side of the arc touches the gourd. I then draw a second arc at this distance from the first and continue to draw more arcs using this measure," Comerford says.

Her design consists of squiggle radiating out from the center of a circle, so she draws pie-wedge lines from the circle's center out to the last arc. "These lines will guide my cuts with the gouge. Before beginning to carve, I settle the gourd securely in my lap on a mat of rubber. I also wear a leather bicycle glove to protect the hand that holds the gourd," Comerford says.

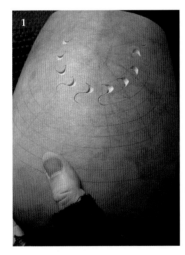

Each chip consists of a stop-cut and a sweep-out. Make the stop-cut by holding the gouge perpendicular to your guideline and press straight down to pierce the gourd shell and dig into the surface (about the depth or thickness of a penny). The result will be a backward C.

Comerford does a row of stop-cuts facing in the same direction. Then she does all the sweep-cuts for that row. The sweep-cut can be made with the gouge blade ¹/₄ inch from and parallel to the curve of the stop-cut. She pierces the shell and wiggles the blade with a gentle rocking wrist motion toward the stop-cut. When the sweep-cut nearly reaches the stop-cut, she removes the blade and cuts the stop-cut slightly deeper. This ensures that no nicks will remain with the finished sweep-cut when the chips are removed.

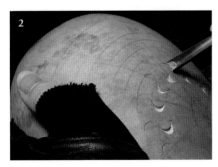

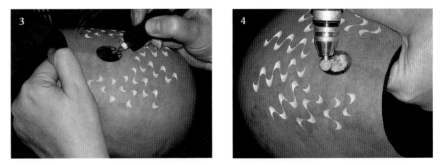

For the second row, make stop-cuts that go in the opposite direction. Each end point should face an end point from the previous row, along the pie-wedge lines. Joining all the stop-cuts back and forth along the pie-wedge lines creates the look of relief squiggles.

For the area to be inlaid with stone, she draws around the stone with a pencil. She uses a wood-burning tool to outline and make checkerboard cuts in the area to be removed. With a rotary hand tool, she carves away the gourd shell slowly so as not to remove too much.

COMPLETE BOOK OF GOURD CARVING

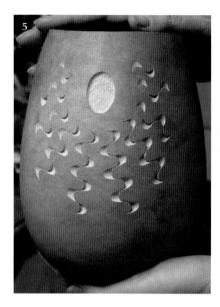

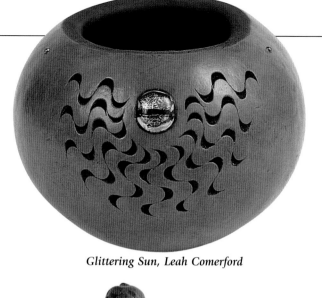

The gourd is now ready to color.

Glittering Sun, Leah Comerford

To prep the gourd for color, wash and dry the outer shell to remove pencil lines. The inner shell can be damp.

With a fine watercolor brush, put a drop of India ink into each chipped area. Moisture left from washing attracts the ink. Clean any stray ink spots with a Q-tip soaked in bleach or turpenoid.

Finally, color the gourd with Dr. Ph. H. Martin's Hydrus fine-art watercolors.

Comerford sets the stone into the inlay cavity with a two-part epoxy.

Birdhouse, Eugene Endicott. Endicott colored the gouge work with India Ink.

Desert Jasper, Leah Comerford

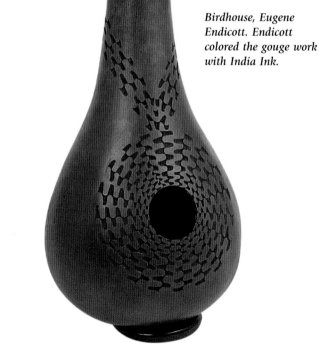

Walter Reinhard

Walter Reinhard has worked with Leslie Miller using gouge tools on a wide variety of gourds. He continues to experiment with different designs, using favorite gouges, and generously shares hints and instructions with beginning gourd carvers. When embellishing birdhouses, he adapts his design to fit many different gourd shapes. For these pet projects, he has used three gouges: #11, ³⁄₁₆-inch; #8, ³⁄₈-inch; and #11, ⅛-inch.

Linking Chains, Walter Reinhard

INLAY & PINEAPPLE PATTERNS

Bronii Williams

"By using beautiful Australian opals, I've combined chip carving and inlay to create exciting designs," gourd artist Bronii Williams says. "I have tried to create many different effects using the gouge. One of these, a linking pattern, involves alternately positioning the stop-cuts along opposite sides of a single line and then using a short sweep-cut with a slightly narrower gouge to create the image of a wavy line. Another style of linking design requires placing a continuous row of stop-cuts on both sides of the line but opposite each other. The pattern becomes one of joined beads or links in a chain.

"To create the scallop effect around the opal inlay, I use a long-handled, #8-sweep, ¼-inch gouge to make the stop-cuts around the carved inlay oval. I then use a slightly narrower gouge to make the sweep-cuts on the outside of the oval, creating a frame effect to set off the stone."

Opal Eye, Bronii Williams

Williams has another pattern she calls the Pineapple series because the surface reminds her of designs she crocheted years ago.

With a fine-line paintbrush, drops of colored leather dye can be added to these chips to enhance the design. "To color the unchipped surfaces, I very quickly apply colored dye and wipe the excess away from surfaces I want left plain with methylated spirits." After the gourd is colored, she finishes it by using clear polyurethane sealer.

Pineapple of Your Eye, Bronii Williams
Collection of Linda Jasper.

Pineapple prep, Bronii Williams

GOUGE
DESIGNS

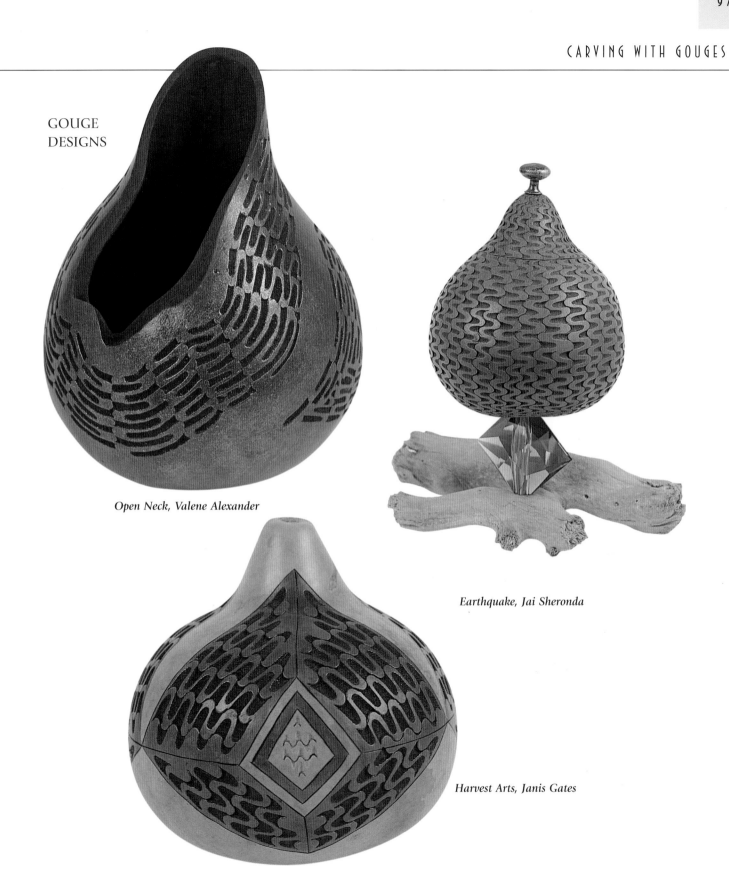

Open Neck, Valene Alexander

Earthquake, Jai Sheronda

Harvest Arts, Janis Gates

NAZCA LINES, GUIRO & PINWHEEL GOUGE DESIGNS

Tito Medina

These images were inspired by the designs of the Nazca lines on the high plateaus of Peru. Tito Medina first carved the images using the gouge; then he chipped the outlines using a chisel. He wanted the surface to remain rough to resemble the desert.

Nazca Lines

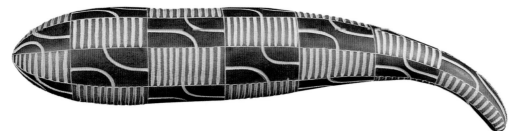

Checkerboard Club. Medina's dyed then gouge-carved club gourd has a pleasing checkerboard pattern.

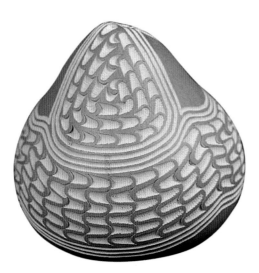

Squiggle Sampler

Quilt. Here is a quilt of intersecting gouge lines.

Guiro

The guiro is an ancient gourd rasp, a musical instrument popular in Afro-Cuban music. The musician plays the guiro by rubbing a stick or thin metal rod rhythmically across the instrument's grooves to produce a washboardlike percussion sound. Making grooves in the gourd shell is easy with the V-gouge.

Make several passes, each time going a little deeper with the gouge rather than trying to make the cut in a single pass. The distance between grooves and the depth of the cut determine the guiro's sound as well as the type and part of the stick rubbed against it.

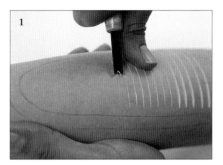

Tito Medina uses the #39, 6-mm V-tool to make a series of shallow, parallel V-grooves evenly spaced.

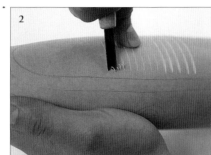

Here is the end of the cut.

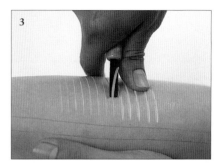

Medina uses the #39, 6-mm V-tool to make shallow grooves deeper.

Medina finishes the cut.

Here is the carved and burned guiro.

Here is the finished guiro with grooves as well as decoration. Tito Medina has achieved six different shades of brown to black, with five shades visible in this photo. He did all shading with the heat of a glowing ember that he carefully manipulated against the gourd shell.

Pinwheel Motif

The pinwheel motif can be a good beginner's exercise. Use a #6, 8-mm straight gouge.

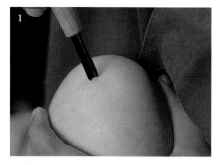

Push the #6, 8-mm straight gouge perpendicularly into the gourd to create a stop-cut.

Reinsert the gouge at an angle ⅛ inch from the first cut and slice toward the stop-cut. Remove the chip.

Note the shape of the cut after removing the chip.

Turn the gourd 180 degrees and make another stop-cut opposite the first one. Then insert the gouge at an angle ⅛ inch from the stop-cut and slice toward the stop-cut. Remove the chip.

Turn the gourd 90 degrees and make another stop-cut and slice.

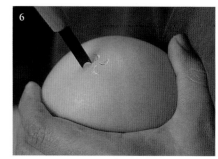

Turn the gourd 180 degrees and repeat the cuts.

Remove the slice.

Continue making stop-cuts and slices until the pinwheel looks complete.

Tito Medina's Gouge Techniques

Here Medina shows how he develops a pattern on the gourd and demonstrates the difference between the wiggle-cut and a straight push-cut.

Using a #6, 8-mm straight gouge, insert the gouge at a slight angle into the gourd skin. Wiggle the gouge to the right while slightly pushing it forward.

Now wiggle the gouge to the left while slightly pushing the gouge in a forward direction.

Now wiggle the gouge to the right while slightly pushing the gouge in a forward direction.

Wiggle the gouge to the left and right. Continue wiggling left and right until the wiggle line is completed. Notice the texture of the gouged arc.

The second arc, the one to the right in the photo, was gouged not with the wiggle-cut but with a straight pushing of the gouge. Notice how the texture of the arc to the right is smoother than the texture of the arc to the left.

Make a stop-cut.

Insert the gouge ¼ inch from the convex side of the stop-cut and push toward the stop-cut to make a thin crescent moon.

Continue to make a series of crescents.

Begin making a series of crescents facing the opposite direction and midway between the previous row of crescents.

The second row of crescents is half done.

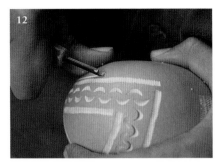

The rows of crescents are surrounded by a wiggle-line border. Then Medina uses a V-gouge to carve a parallel straight line.

A pair of straight lines has been cut with a straight pushing of the V-gouge, as compared with the wiggle-cut previously made.

Using a very shallow sweep gouge, make several lines of the wiggle-cut for texture.

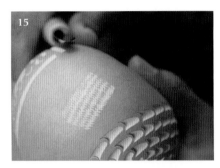

Notice the texture of the wiggle-cut made with a shallow sweep gouge.

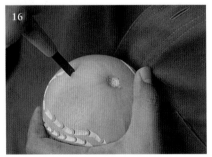

Make the stop-cut.

Wiggle-carve toward the convex side of the stop-cut to make a series of cuts in a spiral around the gourd.

Here is the finished spiral motif.

A third motif with shallow circular depressions is added inside the figure by making short cuts with the larger and deeper gouge.

After three rows of larger depressions, Medina switches to a narrower gouge and continues to make several rows of smaller depressions.

He finishes with an even narrower gouge for the final texture in the center of the figure.

Here is the completed figured motif.

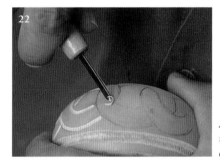

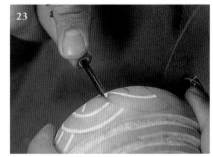

After penciling in the pattern of intersecting arcs, Medina uses a narrow veiner gouge to inscribe the arcs.

In relief carving, the many textures of gourd shell layers can be incorporated into the design.

RELIEF CARVING

$\mathcal{B}$y carving away larger areas of the epidermal layers, the artist can take advantage of the many textures in the different layers of gourd shell and incorporate them into the overall design.

When planning relief carving, consider two options. You can either remove the epidermal layer surrounding the design or carve the design itself into the shell.

If you remove the epidermal layer that surrounds the design, you can provide a framework or a contrast to emphasize the design created on the shell. The design can be left plain so that the texture contrast itself provides the definition. The texture of the exposed inner gourd shell can be finished in many ways, from sanding it smooth to leaving it rough, creating a very irregular textural contrast to the smooth external shell. The carved background may be dyed or stained, so that both the color and textural contrasts help focus the viewer's attention. Artists may choose to enhance their designs with paints, dyes, wood-burning, or inlay. The removed background provides further depth to frame the focal point. Either way, the attention is directed to the design on the foreground surface.

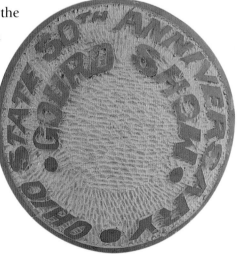

The design itself may be carved into the shell. If the gourd shell has been dyed or colored before carving, the design will provide a pale relief against a darkened background. For this effect, carve the gourd first; then dye or stain it. The pattern will appear as a darkened silhouette against the lighter external surface.

Members of the Fulani tribe in northern Nigeria carved this gourd plaque.
Commissioned by the Ohio State Gourd Society for its 50th anniversary celebration.

John Martin

This project, Butterflies, shows a design where the background was carved away from the images on the external shell. After the carving was completed, the gourd was dyed. The soft inner shell of the background absorbs more dye and is darker.

Butterflies

Strawberry Vase

The design itself of this Strawberry Vase was carved, and the exterior shell remains as the background. John Martin dyed the gourd prior to carving so that the soft inner shell appears light against the darker shell.

For Stencil Bowl, Martin carved the design into the shell and then dyed the entire gourd.

Stencil Bowl

Ginger Summit

Summit's bowls were carved to illustrate the contrast between carving that removes the image, and carving that removes the background of the design. This design was inspired by Mayan hieroglyphs of the heron. Also note the contrast found in John Martin's artwork on p.106 (opposite).   *Mayan Hieroglyphs*

ADINKRA

Jill Walker

Technique of Removing Background

For centuries, the Ashante people in central Ghana have been embellishing fabric, called Adinkra cloth, using stamps made out of gourd shards. The symbols, used specifically for this purpose, evolved over hundreds of years; they represent concepts, stories, parables, individuals, or events in history. Traditionally, the clothing was worn for the funerals of important people in the society. Community members enlisted artists to create textiles, using stamps that referred to important characteristics of the deceased. This cloth was worn for funeral events and a period of mourning. Gradually, these symbols have been combined or adapted so that the repertoire of designs and variations is now up to 400 to 500. Designs originally used only for very limited occasions now grace printed fabrics, many objects for home décor, and even public buildings and flags.

Artists still specialize in traditional printing of Adinkra cloth, using stamps carved out of gourd shells.

After the artist removes the background of the design, he adds a handle to the gourd shard with three or four bamboolike skewers stuck into corners and the other ends tied into a bundle with string or tape. The artist divides the cloth into sections and applies dye with a hair comb. Then he fills in each row or square with a stamped design. Artists originally made dyes by boiling down special leaves and plant material, but today most use commercial dyes and paints.

Creating the Adinkra Stamp

1

For the Adinkra design, transfer a photocopy image onto the gourd shard with the Hot Tool transfer tip. Or draw the image on the gourd with a pencil. The Nkinkyn symbol represents strength, adaptability, and devotion to service.

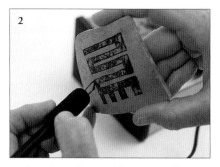

With a Razertip wood-burning tool, cut deep incisions around the outer edge of the design, making it smooth and sharp.

With a #8 sweep, ¼-inch hand gouge, trim away shell surrounding the design. Cut toward the design, stopping just before you reach the wood-burned line. The gourd shell chip will pop out and leave a nice sharp edge around the design.

Use a veiner to remove the background from narrower parts. Sharp garden shears can snip away extra gourd shell and leave a stamp with a carved background that encircles a crisp design for your fabric stamp.

To transfer textile paint or dye onto the stamp, use soft material, such as a cotton rag, sponge, or pad of paper towels. Or paint colors directly onto the stamp with a brush. Try to avoid lumps of paint around edges. To make sure the textile paint or dye sets into the fabric, follow the paint or dye manufacturer's directions. Otherwise, the color may run if the fabric gets wet.

Adinkra stamps on a piece of Adinkra cloth from Ghana, Africa.

CARVED RELIEF BACKGROUND TEXTURING

If you carve away the outer epidermis, you can create contrasting texture with the smooth outer shell. Use hand or power tools.

Tito Medina

Creating Textured Background Using Hand Tools

After Medina carved the linear design in the red-dyed gourd, he used his handmade small, flat chisel to carve away background adjacent to his linear carving.

The finished gourd with background relief.

Here is the guiro (also see pp. 98–99), carved with designs inspired by Nazca lines found in the high plateaus of Peru. Each design was colored a different shade with a burning ember. Background texture surrounding each image helps further distinguish the designs.

The background of the horse shape is created by linear carving with a narrow #9 gouge. A gap left between the lines creates the effect of many different radiating squares around the horse. The linear gouge lines adjacent to the lizard are placed right next to each other, removing all the external shell. This creates a completely different background effect.

The shell surrounding the hummingbird was removed with a wide #8 gouge, using a shallow scooping motion without a stop-cut. The effect created is a surface of gentle rounded shapes. The background surrounding the monkey's tail was created by making very short cuts with a chisel blade resulting in a very rough texture.

Creating Textured Background Using Power Tools

Ginger Summit

Try using power tools to create a variety of background textures in the gourd's soft inner shell. For her Koi Pond gourd, koi fish featured on this gourd swim through a background of swirling water, water plants, and a rough, gravelly pond floor. The kois' outlines were carved using a narrow #9 hand gouge, and the fish were darkened with an orange leather dye. Scales were added with a wider #7 gouge. Summit, using many different bits, carved the background with a power rotary carver.

Koi Pond

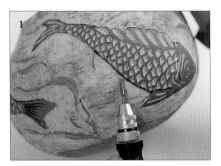

The swirling water effect was carved with an elongated cone with a Kutzall surface (the burr resembles a hedgehog). "This tool creates an extremely rough texture appropriate for this design element," Summit says.

To carve areas immediately around the designs, such as fish and seaweed, a short cylinder was used to make a nice sharp edge.

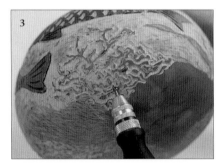

Summit created the gravelly bottom by bouncing different sizes of ball-tip cutting bits on the gourd surface. The different sizes of bits helped create the look of coarse gravel interspersed with sandy areas. Round bits helped suggest underwater coral; instead of bouncing the tip, Summit just wiggled it around the surface.

She created the illusion of sea grass by lightly brushing the ball-tip cutter in a single direction along the gourd's surface.

After the carving was complete, the fish were colored with leather dyes and varnished to create a glossy finish. The water and pond bottom were colored with Ukrainian egg dyes. Because these dyes are water-based, it is easy to dilute them to create a wash effect.

portions surrounding the second side of the gourd were carved after it was dyed, which leaves these areas pale.

Calligraphy gourd from China, two views. Collection of Virginia Saunders.

Goose with Salamanders, Mary Wojeck

WOJECK-STYLE CHIP-RELIEF CARVING

Terry Holdsclaw

Terry Holdsclaw carves with hand tools, following Wojeck-style chip-carving techniques.

Decades ago, Mary Wojeck and her husband, Frank, began using this technique and sharing it with other artists in North Carolina. First the Wojecks cleaned the gourd and sketched the design on the exterior. After deciding which shell portions were to be removed, they marked them with an "X". Then with the carving knife, they delineated the outer lines of the design and both rims. They cut horizontal lines about 1 mm apart into the gourd shell in all the portions to be removed. Then they cut vertical lines in all these areas to create hatch marks over the previously cut horizontal lines. After scoring the lines, the Wojecks used a knife blade to pick out all the little squares, which removed the exterior shell and created a background for the design. After finishing the gourd as desired, they treated it with a polyurethane spray.

Maple Leaves

Maple Leaves detail, with knife.

*Leaves of plants native to North Carolina
and Tennessee.*

Japanese Maple Leaves

*Maple Leaves and Seeds, native to North
Carolina and Tennessee.*

USING SANDBLASTER FOR RELIEF CARVING

Jim Strand

Jim Strand has been using a very fine, directed sand-blaster to carve intricate designs in stones. It seemed like a viable technique for gourds, so we gave him some gourds to experiment with and he came back to show us his technique. First he photocopies his design onto a vellum negative. Then he makes a photo mask applied to the stone or, in this case, gourd. The mask, which is resilient to a stream of particles, covers the pattern areas that are to remain. Jim can control the carving depth and thus produce layers of relief as well as control the texture.

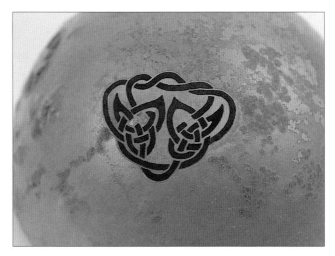

Celtic Knot, Jim Strand. The photo mask stencil protects the areas that are to remain.

Crown Shakra Lotus detail.

Bamboo

Seven Spirals

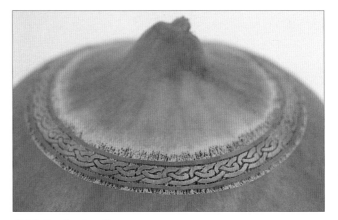

Celtic Border detail.

Mary Segreto

Mary Segreto explains her technique: "I usually use a simple design along with a fine finish to highlight my carved gourds. Only elbow grease using fine, super-fine, and micro-fine sanding pads and clear wax were used to accent the leaf carving. I use a Dremel tool with a flexible shaft and a 2.3-mm reverse taper high-speed cutting bit to outline my relief carvings. Once the outline is completed, I use the same cutter as a router bit to undercut around the pattern and begin removing the background material. For a smooth background, I prefer using the top end of a larger cylindrical cutter, using it as a small router for clean removal of material. A ball-tip cutter is used for a rough or dimpled finish in a size appropriate to the pattern."

Birthmark with Leaves. The naturally occurring blotch on the gourd reminded Segreto of a birthmark.

Oak Leaves

Geometric Braid

A POTPOURRI OF RELIEF-CARVING TECHNIQUES

Rhoda Forbes

For Eagles Flying, Rhoda Forbes drew the design free-hand, wood-burned it, and applied cordovan leather dye to the whole gourd. Using a high-speed rotary carver with an engraving bit, she carved around the design. Pine-needle coiling finishes the design.

Fertile Nights was carved with a very small U-gouge and V-gouge. Forbes dyed the gourd with leather dye and sketched the design with white charcoal pencil.

Eagles Flying, Rhoda Forbes

Gwen Heineman

Poppies also uses relief carving and leather dye.

Fertile Nights, Rhoda Forbes

Poppies, Gwen Heineman

Paul Klopfenstein

"I draw my designs on the gourd freehand with pencil and wood-burn the design," gourd artist Paul Klopfenstein says. "Afterward, I add the colors. When the colors are dry, I spray the gourd with clear acrylic sealer to set the colors and protect them from possible damage when carving. Then I use the Turbocarver II to carve out the background, using a variety of dental burrs. For a final finish, I use a matte acrylic sealer with an ultraviolet inhibitor."

Lidded bowl, Paul Klopfenstein

Lidded bowl detail, Paul Klopfenstein.

Andre Nigoghossian

Andre Nigoghossian began Dragon as a demonstration piece at the Zittel Gourd Festival. He used the MiniCraft high-speed drill with a ball-tip cutter to remove the background. For removing the remainder of the background, he found it faster to work with a gouge, creating a texture with the wiggle-cut.

Dragon, Andre Nigoghossian

Susan Levesque

Gourd artist Susan Levesque's design for Poppies was transferred to this cannonball gourd by using a template. She adds details by hand. Levesque explains her technique: "I use a technical pen with black India ink to put the detail into my design. Then I use a Dremel carver with the flexible shaft to complete the carving. I use the small engraving cutters at a medium to high speed. (1) I start with a #24967, which has a carving point of ³⁄₃₂ inch, to cut through the outer shell and get most of the rough work done. (2) I then change to a #106 with a carving point of ¹⁄₁₆ inch to clean a nice edge around the pattern and smooth things out. (3) Finally, I change to a #24950, which has a carving point of ¹⁄₃₂ inch, to get into the tiny corners and bring out the details. After the carving is finished, I apply two to three coats of a matte sealer to protect the finish of the gourd." (Numbers refer to Dremel product codes.)

Jungle Stripes, Kathy Doolittle

Kathy Doolittle

Kathy Doolittle penciled in the design for Jungle Stripes and followed the pencil marks with a woodburner. She then applied cordovan leather dye over the gourd's entire surface. Using a small round carving burr, she carved out the pattern and then painted the exposed surface with acrylics.

Poppies, Susan Levesque

Karen Cheeseman

"For the past five years, my husband has been growing gourds on our farm in midwestern Ontario. I do almost all my carving with a Dremel tool with a flexible shaft. I use high-speed cutters from both Dremel and my dentist, ranging in size from ³⁄₁₆ inch down to ¹⁄₃₂ inch. I also use a scalpel knife for some cutting. I usually transfer designs onto the gourds and then carve them. I use colored waxes on the gourds, and all my pieces are sealed with three to four coats of paste floor wax," Karen Cheeseman says.

Leaves with green wax, Karen Cheeseman.

CHINESE GOURDS BY THE MIAO

These decorated gourds are from the Dong people, Guizhou province in southern China. They were carved by the Miao (Meo, Hmoung) people before 1990.

Background (negative space) has been carved away around the Chinese characters. Mei Han Collection. Photo courtesy of Randy Raine-Reusch.

The background is carved away to reveal the dancing figures on the gourd shell. Mei Han Collection. Photo courtesy of Randy Raine-Reusch.

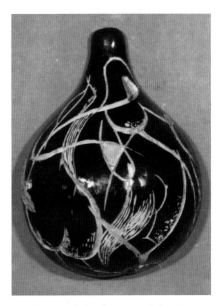

On this gourd the foreground (positive space) has been carved away to create the pattern. Mei Han Collection. Photo courtesy of Randy Raine-Reusch.

Kimo Truman

"For all my projects, I first sketch the design on the gourd and then burn in the design using the Detail Master burning system," Kimo Truman says. "I then carve around the design with a Dremel or a Miyad electric carving system, using the large, medium, and small ball-tips, or cylinder burrs. I work the surface around the design to create a three-dimensional look. When this is completed, I spray with clear enamel paint (eight to ten coats)."

Chosen One

Hawaiian Canoe Paddler

Rain Forest Orangutan

Nativity

Lorraine Zielinski

The gourd Nativity was done with the basic technique of carving the image itself into a solidly dyed gourd. "All my work," Lorraine Zielinski says, "starts with the idea stage, and then detailed drawings are done before I transfer the work to the surface of the gourd, using carbon paper. Sometimes after I transfer the design, I burn it into the gourd before I begin carving.

"For the carving itself, I use a high-speed rotary carver with a flexible shaft. Most of the bits I use are the round carving bits from 1/16 up to 1/8 inch. I prefer to use the flexible shaft because it gives me a pencillike feel and the control I need to carve intricate designs. The size of the area to be carved and the amount of detail is what determines the size of bit used. For the relief carving, the texture is obtained by simply touching the surface of the gourd with the bit at high speed. For the gourds that have artwork carved into them, I may stain the gourd first, then transfer the design."

Horses

Eileen Marcotte

To create her whimsical artwork, Eileen Marcotte begins with a gourd that has been completely cleaned, inside and out. She then pencils on the design and wood-burns the marks. The surfaces that will not be removed by carving she colors with leather dyes or acrylics. After the colors are completely dry, she uses a Dremel tool with a flexible shaft and a variety of tips. "I usually carve a small portion at a time and then give my hands a rest. I have found that carving away from the normal circular flow of the tip rotation seems to help in control," Marcotte says. "Finally, I touch up any color that has been chipped away with the high-speed rotary carver."

Mom, Dad, and the Kids (giraffes)

I'm Thinking of Cutting My Hair (mask)

Party of Five (zebras)

Linda Evaro

First, Linda Evaro draws the design on the gourd and then uses a hobby knife with a concave blade to carve away the background for her designs. After she completes all carving, she washes the gourd with warm soapy water to remove any pencil marks. The carving leaves a corklike texture in the background that is either painted or stained with acrylic paints. The designs on the gourd's surface are also painted with acrylic paints. Then the entire gourd is treated with a clear acrylic spray.

Medicine Man Circle detail with knife used for carving.

Medicine Man Circle

Desert scene with painted background.

Bill Colligen

Bill Colligen uses a wood-burner to engrave the design into the gourd shell. "This makes it easier to accomplish minute detail when carving around the design. I am less likely to gouge into the areas I want to retain, and it also provides a clean edge. I start carving out the larger areas with a drum sander or a typhoon (also known as a Kutzall) rotary burr, depending on the density of the area. Then I use a reverse tapered diamond burr to get into the very small areas. Sometimes I finish these areas with a #2 hobby knife by deepening the burn line and going underneath the area to be removed with the knife tip." To finish smoothing out the removed area, Colligen uses various round diamond burrs. Using a 3/16-inch round diamond burr, he creates a textured surface.

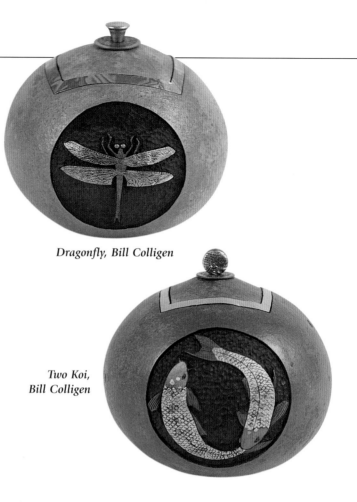

Dragonfly, Bill Colligen

Two Koi,
Bill Colligen

Cyndee Newick

To create the Wishing Well, Cyndee Newick wood-burned the stone outlines with a standard skew tip. Using a high-speed rotary carver with a small round ball-tip cutter, she removed wider sections. To make narrow channels, Newick wood-burned deeper. She wood-burned roof shingles and sponge-painted the stones with many different colors. Finally, she painted the roof with a brush to produce the impression of moss-covered shingles.

Wishing Well,
Cyndee Newick

C. Siles Molina

After sketching the design on the gourd, C. Siles Molina carves with a high-speed drill and a spherical ⅛-inch bit. Next he uses inks to color the designs. Finally, he uses a coat of varnish to protect the paints.

Hawaiian Flowers

Manini Convict Fish

Hawaiian Flowers, detail.

Cass Iverson

For gourd carving, Cass Iverson uses several burrs
with a high-speed drill. A finish, which she originated, uses different types of novelty paints. She first
carves and then paints the entire gourd, inside and
out, with a textured paint. After it dries, she sponges
on a second lighter shade, carefully keeping the
carved areas darker. The effect is a pottery bowl with
carved relief.

Mayan Bowl

Celtic Bowl

Canyon de Chelly Petroglyphs

Ronna Wuttke

To create the work Out of Africa, Ronna Wuttke used an Ultima tool with a small ball-tip cutter for cutting close to the Optima wood-burned lines. She used a larger ball-tip cutter for removing larger areas. On this very thick gourd, she penciled the outline, wood-burned the drawing, carved out the background, and finally painted the piece.

Out of Africa, Ronna Wuttke. Giraffes were wood-burned; the background was painted. Photo by Derral Durrence.

Out of Africa, Ronna Wuttke. The elephant in the foreground was carved with some depth. Photo by Derral Durrence.

Kris Mangliers

To give definition to the feathers around the neck of her bowl, Kris Mangliers uses relief carving.

Feathers Bowl, Kris Mangliers

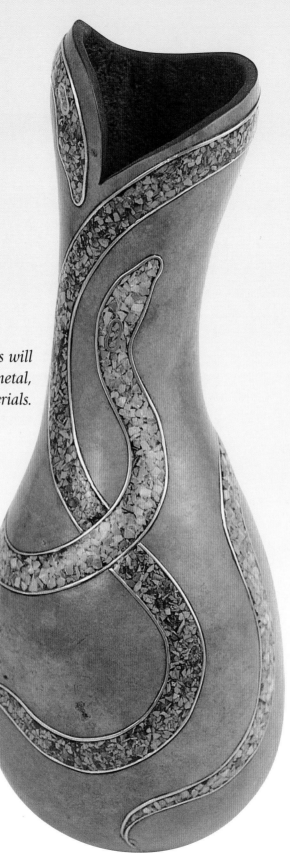

Only dense, sturdy gourds will support inlays of stone, metal, shells, or other materials.

INLAY TECHNIQUES

$\mathcal{F}$or centuries, artisans have set stones, metal, or shells into gourd surfaces. Ancient gourds, often embellished by inlaid pieces of mother-of-pearl, were the property of tribal chiefs or clan leaders; many were used as containers that held sacred objects or were themselves used in ceremonies. Adding precious materials to the gourd itself signified its value. (The gourd Pelicans, found in ancient Peru, features inlaid abalone shell; see p. 6.)

Today artists blend a wide variety of materials into gourd shells to create unusual and highly decorative pieces. The embedded or inlaid objects may be as simple as sand, pebbles, or broken china, or as valuable as semiprecious stones and metals. The gourd shell provides a sturdy and novel structural framework adaptable to any style.

For inlay projects, it's important to choose a sturdy, thick gourd. The shell thickness, of course, depends on the material to be embedded and the depth it is to be set. For some objects, such as cabochon stones, metal foils, or snakeskin, it is enough simply to remove the slick outer shell so that the adhesive bonds with the more porous inner shell. For designs where you want the object's face mounted flush with the gourd's surface, you'll need a very thick shell. In both cases, the shell should be dense. Some gourds with thick shells are still quite light because of the inner shell's porosity or softness. Even thick, soft shells can become brittle and crack when dry.

First, prepare the shell and plan the overall design. If the inlay is a single element in a larger design, do other tasks first, such as wood-burning and texturing. Place the object to be inset on the gourd shell, and draw around it as closely and accurately as possible. Remove the gourd shell's outer surface with hand or power tools, testing frequently to make sure the object fits snugly. After the surface is carved to a sufficient depth, many artists like to dye or paint supplementary designs at this stage. Otherwise, glue the object or material in the carved area with strong craft glue. Some artists prefer a two-part epoxy. When the adhesive is dry, fill any holes around the object with caulking. Many different products are appropriate for this, such as wood putty, which comes in many shades of brown and other colors. Or combine gourd sawdust with white glue to fill in any extra cracks; this mixture dries to become almost invisible on the gourd shell.

Complete the design when the object is securely seated and spaces are filled in. You may want to protect the inlaid object's surface with drafting tape so that stray dyes or paints do not mar its surface.

CREATING SEMIPRECIOUS STONE & WIRE INLAYS

Ginger Summit

Hopi Butterfly Dancers

Hopi Butterfly Dancers uses two types of inlays: a turquoise stone and copper wire. However, a seemingly limitless variety of materials will work for inlays. Adapt these steps to fit any need.

Hopi Butterfly Dancers

Wood-burn the design on the gourd, and paint parts of the design with black and turquoise enamel and antique copper metallic paint. Don't worry about painting outside the lines at this stage.

Remove the background surrounding the dancers, or other figures you want to introduce, with a ball-tip burr in a rotary carver.

Put the turquoise stone on the gourd where it is to be set, and carefully trace around it with a pencil.

Carve out the area to make an indentation for the stone. Test frequently so that the stone fits the carved space as exactly as possible. It's much easier to carve a tight fit than to try to fill gaps later.

Glue the turquoise into the recessed area with strong hobby glue. Some artists prefer to use a two-part epoxy, available in small quantities in dual vials.

Just below the black line around the gourd's midline, carve a thin groove around the gourd, using a cutter narrower than the width of the copper wire for the inlay. Use a small ball-tip cutter to adjust the groove width so that the wire will fit snugly.

If you first wood-burn the line, it will be easier to guide the rotary carver.

Glue a copper wire into the grooves at the design's top and bottom, again using a strong glue or epoxy. Masking tape is sometimes necessary to hold the material in place while the adhesive dries.

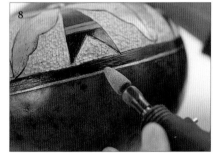

Because the rounded surface of the copper wire was shiny and protruded slightly from the gourd's surface, Summit flattened it with the sanding tip on the rotary carver.

Summit used leather dye on the bottom and neck. To reflect the inlaid turquoise stone and integrate the design, she used turquoise wax on the lower portion of the gourd.

CREATING MOSAIC INLAY USING PORCELAIN

Ginger Summit

Porcelain or colorful ceramic chips set in cement stepping stones, garden pots, or other outdoor décor are appealing. Why not try using these chips on a gourd?

"The first step was to break colorful cups and plates (not my best china, of course) into small chunks. I did this outside, wearing goggles and gloves. By smashing the pieces inside a large cardboard box, I prevented the shards from flying away and posing a health risk to others," Summit says. "Next I threw out all pieces without colors on them and separated the remaining chunks into colors and styles, such as flowers, borders, lines, and solid colors."

Summit chose a very thick gourd with a fairly flat surface. A smaller gourd would have been too curved to match the slightly curved porcelain chips. She sketched the area she wanted removed and used a rotary power tool with a coarse-grit cylinder-drum sander to grind the deep portions.

She first filled in the area with air-drying clay, and while it was still wet, she pressed the china chips into the clay. Then she made a moist slip from clay and water, which she rubbed over the entire inlay. This filled all spaces between the chips.

In part of the design, several larger chunks of china spilled over into the body of the gourd. Summit drew an outline around each chunk.

She then routed out these areas with a rotary carver ball-tip. When she completed grinding, she glued each piece in place.

After the entire design was finished, the clay was allowed to dry and the extra pieces of china were glued in place. She again made a thin slip of clay and water and covered the entire gourd, making sure to fill any gaps and cracks in the dried clay.

Some china pieces still had sharp edges that protruded from the clay, so the gourd was sanded with several different grits of sanding pads, taking care not to sand the images off the china.

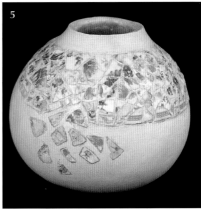

After the edges were rounded smooth, the gourd was painted with white latex paint. Several coats of wax and furniture polish helped to antique the white surface.

Shell & Glass Variations on Porcelain Inlays

Coconut shell inlay, Ginger Summit.

Inlaid handmade glass set into depressions, hand carved with Japanese gouges, Leigh Adams.

CREATING INLAYS WITH INLACE EPOXY

Cindy Lee

Pre-Columbian Kingfisher

Pre-Columbian Kingfisher

For carving gourds, Cindy Lee prefers a pneumatic carving tool. Its high rpm cuts very smoothly through the gourd shell with tips that have ¹⁄₁₆-inch shafts and steel-carbide heads. To create the Pre-Columbian Kingfisher bowl, Lee applies a light wood stain to the gourd and then draws the design freehand with a pencil.

With a tapered fine-tip carbide cutter, she carves along all these lines to establish a good, clean line.

Using several different sizes of ball-tips, Lee removes the gourd shell within the lines. After carving, she smoothes the edges lightly with sandpaper or a small round file.

Kathi Klopfenstein

Votive Candleholder

For her Votive Candleholder gourd, Kathi Klopfenstein first wood-burned the design and then sponge-painted it with acrylic paints. Using the spherical tip on the high-speed rotary carver, she made the basic shape of the hole in the gourd shell. She created a ledge to hold the fused glass with a cylinder tip. The glass pieces were then glued in place with craft glue.

Votive Candleholder, Kathi Klopfenstein

John Rizzi

Chipped Semiprecious Stone Inlays

These elegant gourds are inlaid with a variety of chipped semiprecious stones, outlined with sterling silver wire. Although the process sounds simple, the results are gourds of exceptional beauty.

First, artist John Rizzi carves two trenches just wide enough to hold the silver wire. The wire is then glued into the carved lines with superglue. After the glue is completely set, Rizzi carves out the spaces between the two silver trenches with a rotary carver and a tiny inverted cone. He crushes semiprecious stones in an iron skillet with a hammer and then sets them in the carved spaces with superglue. After the glue has cured and the crushed stone is firmly set, he smoothes the surface with a coarse sanding drum attached to a high-speed drill. Finally, he hand sands the gourds with five grades of sanding pads to achieve a highly polished surface.

Caution: It's important to always wear a mask and use a filtered exhaust system to draw away the dust. Both the superglue and the dust of the semiprecious stones are highly toxic.

Tibetan turquoise inlay, John Rizzi.

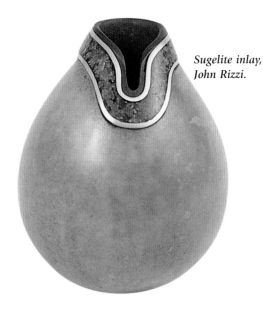

Sugelite inlay, John Rizzi.

Ginger Summit

For Hopi Feathers, Summit crushed turquoise stones with a hammer in a metal pot. She put a two-part resin in the carved areas and pressed in the turquoise firmly. After the resin was set, she sanded the gourd with a drum sander. Finally, she carefully inlaid silver wire around the neck of the design.

*Hopi Feathers, pattern in turquoise,
Ginger Summit.*

*Turquoise Kokopelli,
Tim Boland*

Tim Boland

The bird perched in this cage was inlaid with coral, turquoise, and lapis lazuli. The gourd was painted inside and out with white enamel; then it was sanded to produce a mottled surface.

Birdcage, Tim Boland

USING PEBBLES FOR INLAYS

Nancy Miller

Before she begins, Nancy Miller cleans and sands the gourd. "I sand with several different grades of sanding pads so that the final finish is extremely smooth to the touch. The permanent mold stains on the gourd surface often suggest the design. I draw in pencil, connecting the dots of the natural patterns and adding a flourish or two of my own," Miller says.

"I begin routing using a Dremel tool with a flexible shaft and a Typhoon carbide burr, which makes quick work of roughing out the bulk of the design. Then I graduate to a high-speed steel cutter with a flat cylinder bit. I may continue to refine the design with a micro-cutter bit, and the final edging is done with diamond-coated micro-burrs.

"The next step is to dye or paint the cleared area with a dark color that is compatible with the color that I'll eventually use to dye the gourd surface. I prefer to use a Ukranian egg dye for this step because I use a very fine brush and quickly wipe away any dye that gets on the gourd's external surface.

"Before I start the inlay process, I sort the pebbles according to size and color in small trays. I begin by laying down a thumbnail-size area of white glue. (Wellbond glue works best for me.) Then I pick up the pebbles with a toothpick with beeswax on the end

This gourd bowl with inlaid African ostrich eggshell beads and grout was wood-burned, dyed, and polished.

and place them in the glued areas one by one. "After the area is filled with pebbles and the glue has dried, I mix up a small batch of charcoal-colored tile grout and rub it into the spaces between the pebbles. When I have cleaned up from the mess that the grout makes, I use a fine dental pick and a toothbrush or stencil brush to gently take away the grout that has covered some of the shallower pebbles. After the grout has set (at least a day), I dye and polish the gourd."

GOURD PIN WITH OSTRICH EGGSHELL BEADS

The gourd piece has been cut, cleaned, and sanded. Note the pencil drawing of the area to be carved.

The first carving stage is done with the Typhoon carbide burr.

Continue carving with a high-speed steel cutter with a flat end. This helps establish depth and a smooth base.

Finish the edges with a diamond-coated micro-burr.

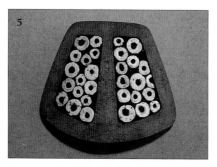

The carved area is dyed dark, and ostrich eggshell beads are glued down with white glue or tacky glue.

Grout has been added to the carved area, and the surrounding gourd surface has been dyed.

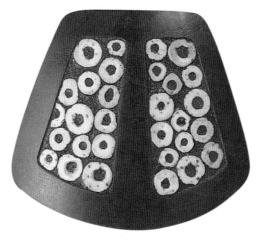

Here is Nancy Miller's finished gourd pin with ostrich eggshell beads.

GOURD PIN WITH STONE BEAD INLAY

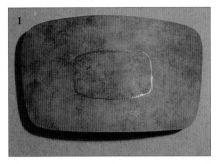

This drawing shows the area to be carved for the stone bead inlay.

The artist carves with a Typhoon burr, along with many other burrs to finish the job.

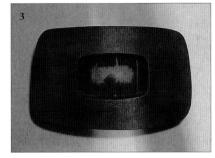

The carved area is dyed dark around the edges so that no pale gourd will show, and the pin's surface is dyed as well.

Two mini-clamps hold the stone in place until the glue sets.

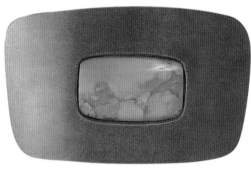

Here is Nancy Miller's finished gourd pin with a stone bead inlay.

Gourd with inlaid pebbles, Nancy Miller.

Nancy Miller's gourd Dripping Pebbles was dyed and polished. Miller put a thin mixture of white glue and water on the grout to prevent it from crumbling.

Dripping Pebbles, Nancy Miller. Photo by John Werner.

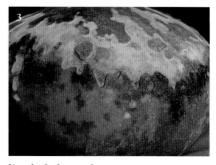

First the design is drawn in pencil on this very large (18-inch) intact gourd.

Carved design with dots or islands. Miller applies dark dye to the cutout areas.

Details of applied dye to the cutout areas.

These inlaid pebbles fill in the cutout areas of the gourd.

GROUT INLAYS

This gourd was carved and then painted black. White grout was rubbed over the surface to completely fill the lines. Before the grout inlay was completely dry, the excess was wiped off with a damp sponge. For spiral cuts, see the chapter "Linear Carving," p. 63.

Grout Swirls,
Ginger Summit

SMALL BOWL WITH GROUT INLAY

Nancy Miller

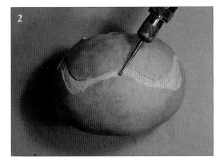

"I use a small steel cutter to carve out the design area. I use the Typhoon burr just a little bit on this piece because the area that could tolerate the roughest burr is very small," Miller says.

She uses a very tiny steel cutter for narrow areas of the design.

For final edging, Miller uses a diamond-coated burr.

Here is the gourd bowl with inlaid grout.

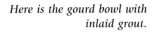

EMU EGGSHELL INLAY

Rob Ghio

For several years, Rob Ghio and his wife have been raising emus, and Rob has been etching emu eggshells. His favorite tool, a pneumatic dental drill, has extremely fine cutting bits that allow excellent control for carving to different depths in the eggshell to reveal the different colored layers. He quickly realized that he could use his carving techniques on gourds to provide a canvas for emu eggshell art.

He uses a Fordham tool for the gourd work. He first wood-burns a line, then carves to the line with a 1/16-inch ball-tip burr. He mostly uses three sizes of ball-tip burrs: the larger burr for the larger areas and the smaller burrs for the smaller areas. He also uses a cylinder, a flame, and an inverted cone for a deeper cut.

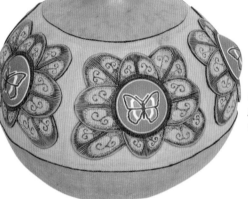

Detail of Five Butterflies.

Five Butterflies. This Indonesian gourd has inlaid and carved emu eggshell.

Bottle gourd detail.

Bottle gourd with inlaid and carved emu eggshell.

OTHER INLAY MATERIALS

Autumn Leaves in suede, Ginger Summit.

Autumn Leaves in copper, Ginger Summit.

Ginger Summit

"I was challenged to use materials with unusual textures to provide a contrast with the gourd surface. Both suede and copper provide textural as well as visually distinct images," Summit says.

This gourd, created by Nancy Miller, has a small square opening and tiny Australian eucalyptus pods inset into holes and woodburned into the gourd shell.

Sculptural carving is useful in drawing attention to a specific area of the design.

DEEP RELIEF OR SCULPTURAL CARVING

A unique feature of carving designs on gourds is that the artist can use the contrasting textures of the hard outer shell and the softer, more porous inner shell to add layers of complexity to the design. For many artists, simply a depressed line or series of spots or gouges can add depth to an otherwise flat image. When the background is carved away, the recession of the surrounding area helps focus attention on a smaller area that stands out in contrast. Or, as illustrated in earlier chapters, the design itself can be cut into the surface and the textures of the inner shell can provide a dimension to the silhouettelike carving.

Some artists take advantage of the gourd's thick shell to create a bas-relief carving. They use the round gourd to provide the sculpture's basic shape, but treat the surface not so much as a canvas but as a hollow block for carving multidimensional designs or patterns. In this category are several distinctive styles of carved gourds. Some remain pictorial, in which carved images are set within a background that has itself been carved and provides a context and setting, rather than just a frame, for the design.

Some shells are thick enough to create almost a completely three-dimensional effect by allowing parts of the image to stand free of the background. When this is not possible, extra dimensionality can be created by undercutting the objects, making them appear to float or be independent of the shell.

A completely different technique makes use of deeply carved and shaped lines that entirely remove the surface outer shell and mold the thick inner shell into new shapes. These gourds almost appear to have been grown in a mold, but the lines and patterns are carved in a way that a mold could not duplicate.

SCULPTURAL CARVING ON A THICK SHELL

Ginger Summit

What's for Lunch? Lizards.

Ginger Summit saves exceptionally thick gourds for sculptural carving. This particular gourd was given to her with the top and seeds removed, but the pulp lining the gourd's interior surface was intact. It was sitting on a patio table with a lizard perched on top, perhaps looking for bugs. A lizard design seemed appropriate, but one lizard soon grew in her imagination into a colony.

What's for Lunch? Lizards.

Summit penciled in the basic design, then drew it with a marking pen on the shell. She used a coarse sanding drum on a high-speed rotary carver to grind away the shell surrounding each lizard.

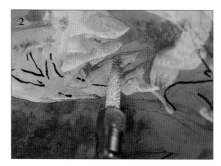

Summit uses a cone-shaped Kutzall grinding tip to grind away the background in smaller spaces, such as between fingers and toes.

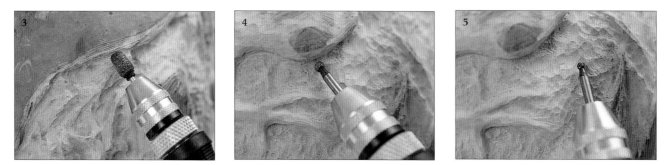

With a variety of carving bits, Summit gradually shapes the lizards and background.

Round sanding caps that fit on rubber cones helped shape and smooth the body of each lizard.

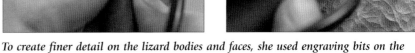

To create finer detail on the lizard bodies and faces, she used engraving bits on the Turbocarver II pneumatic air drill.

When carving the background, Summit often keeps one hand inside the gourd so that she can feel just how close she is to the inner surface. When the drill broke through the surface, she repaired the hole with wood putty.

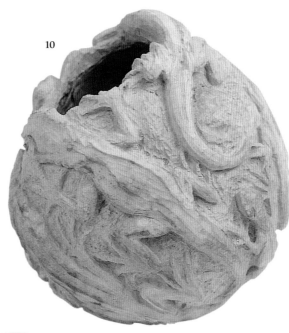

After the lizards were shaped, she smoothed out the background texture of the rocks by using both the ball-tip cutter and sanding tips.

When the carving was complete, she colored the lizards with watercolor dyes, stains, and metallic pigments. A gloss varnish protects the lizards. The background rock surface was colored with watercolor stains and given a final brush with ashes to create a dull granite effect.

Betty Finch

Betty Finch, a master gourd pyro-engraver, has recently been bitten by the carving bug. Using imperfections in the gourd surface as a beginning, Finch will turn these bug cavities and insect scars into mottled landscapes for her wood-burned horse scenes.

Finch sketched the subject for Wistful on the gourd. Then she colored the background areas with bright colored pencils, indicating that they should be ground away. A different colored pencil indicated what areas should have the surface textured but not ground away completely. She used a high-speed rotary carver with a cone-shaped grinding tip.

The subject matter was pyroengraved, starting with objects in the foreground. She added detail with watercolor and colored pencils.

Wistful

Cliff Dwelling

Gophers ate the taproot off the vine this gourd, used for Cliff Dwelling, grew on. The gourd was not mature enough to stay smooth and round as it slowly dehydrated, but the vine stayed alive long enough for the gourd walls to thicken. The hot, dry climate allowed it to shrivel instead of rot. The walls were thick enough to carve away a considerable amount and not break through the shell.

"I first used a flat file to rasp away flat spots for the buildings. Then I used a pocketknife to etch in the path steps and details. An awl was used to shape the windows and doors. The support 'logs' are dried iceplant stems, and the ladders are made of thin slivers of black bamboo," Finch says.

Stella Stewart

Stella Stewart was a wood carver long before she discovered gourds. For Running in the Wind, she used a #3 sweep, ½-inch gouge as well as a ⅛-inch veiner for the carving and a carving knife to clean up the edges. She finished the piece by wiping it with black shoe polish. She has learned that with gourds it's even more important to keep the tools very sharp, because a dull tool will crush the pulpy inner gourd shell rather than cutting it.

Running in the Wind, Stella Stewart

Thelma Dixie Kusche

In the 1940s, Thelma Dixie Kusche was called the Gourd Lady of San Diego. She used only hand carving tools to create these fascinating pieces, now in the collection of David and Ronna Wuttke.

Elephant Hunt, Thelma Dixie Kusche. Photo by Derral Durrence.

Two-Handle Pot, Thelma Dixie Kusche. Photo by Derral Durrence.

Bonnie Leigh

Bonnie Leigh explains her process: "After cleaning and preparing the gourd and before I do any drawing, my best tool is Earthquake putty or mounting putty. Most of the time, I roll the putty out into a rope and drape it to outline where I'm going to cut it and where I want to outline the frame of my carving. This helps me visualize the outlines from a distance before deciding exactly how and where things will appear from all angles of the gourd.

"Then I cut, clean the inside, and begin sketching what I'm going to carve. If a crack appears at this point, I use air-dry clay to fill in. Then I try to use that line or area in part of my design. Usually it works in quite well."

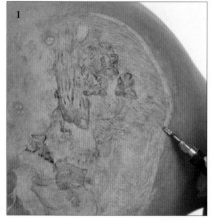

"First I use the Dremel with one of the steel, carbide, or diamond bits, usually beginning at the frame line. Looking at the sketch, I decide where the high and low points will be. When carving you can change the way a line looks just by turning the gourd to the side or upside down. I then do the preliminary sketch with one of the tiny dentist or pointed bits just to break the gourd skin and remove background stock as much as possible. Leave some of the hard shell alone for things such as tree trunks, rocks, etc. The selection of which bit to use is a personal preference." Leigh says. Photo by Sharyn Sakimoto.

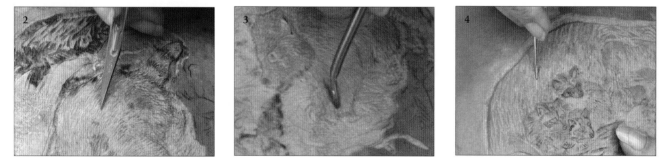

After removing most of the background material, she switches to hand tools, scalpels, and dentists' tools to cut, indent, and smooth. Photo by Sharyn Sakimoto.

After most of the carving is done, Leigh uses power bits made of stone to smooth out backgrounds and feather out the framework. She sometimes uses diamond bits for more back cutting to define separation lines and to simulate depth.

Then she uses a little sandpaper and she's ready for stain or paint. If she decides to leave the surface natural, she seals it with a spray fixative and then a sealer. The kind of sealer she uses depends on the effect she wants. Photo by Sharyn Sakimoto.

Penguins before painting. Photos by Bonnie Leigh.

Penguins after painting. Photos by Chuck Benes.

Marguerite Smith

"Relief carving," Marguerite Smith says, "is a technique that I have become passionate about because it makes the subject matter in my art pieces look more realistic and alive. Everything on my gourds is done freehand; therefore, I usually sketch and plan out my subject matter and sketch it onto the gourd. If the top is to be removed, I clean the inside out without scraping all the pulp totally. This makes a thicker surface to carve. I'll coat the interior with a thick acrylic paint and a heavy coat of varathane. After the interior is dry, the work begins. With a combination of acrylic paints and wood-burning, I create the main artwork."

"I begin to carve out the main and larger areas with my super Dremel," Smith says. *"My favorite tips to remove massive amounts of gourd are the structured-tooth tungsten-carbide cutters, which come in different shapes."*

"I switch to my Powercrafter air-turbine tool, which gives me the ability to carve fine small objects and do undercutting behind the subject matter. A high-speed rotary carver fitted with dental tips would work at this stage also."

After completing most of the carving, I do finish sanding on the gourd by hand and with the high-speed rotary carver. I then add more color to the main design subject and smaller objects. I usually use a combination of acrylics, leather dyes, leather acrylics, silk paint, and crystal clear. I also do wood-burning and cut-burning (a technique of wood-burning).

"The inlaying and weaving of metals can be done at any time. I love the look of copper, stainless, silver, and brass on gourds. The final step is to coat the gourd with a sealer of your choice. I prefer to use water-based Flecto varathane," Smith says.

Friends of Nature. Photo by Paul Smith.

RESCUING FAILED PROJECTS

Ginger Summit

"I always save thick gourds that began their lives as other projects, which subsequently failed. All the following projects started out as something else—wood-burning mistakes, gourds attacked by squirrels, stains that didn't work. By carving deep into the shell of the gourd, you can bypass those errors and often create works of art," Summit explains.

Bouquet of Flowers

Bouquet of Flowers

This gourd started with many flaws—cracks in the skin, warts, and bumps. Flowers provide an extremely flexible way to work around all these problems, turning them into advantages. Another goal is to utilize the entire gourd in the design, including the bottom surface, which is too often ignored.

Close-up of flowers; notice how the carving under the surface of the petals provides depth and delicacy.

Bouquet of Flowers, leaf pattern on the gourd's bottom.

Grape Harvest

Grape Harvest

This gourd was carved and then stained with watercolors and dyes. The leaves and tendrils were undercut with engraving tips to suggest delicacy and depth.

Oriental Treasure Chest

A Chinese carved wooden box seen in a museum long ago inspired this small canteen. The flower motif covers the entire surface of the gourd, including the bottom, which shows roots and little insects in the soil. All carving was done with a turbine rotary carver, using a variety of carving tips. After the carving was completed, the surface was sealed with two coats of natural wood stain and sealer. Then several coats of furniture polish and light scratch remover were rubbed on to provide the shading and depth of the many carved layers.

Oriental Treasure Chest

Rose

This gourd started out with an unsuccessful wood-burned design. "Because it was a lovely thick gourd, I did not want to throw it away, and knew I had to carve somewhat deep into the shell to avoid the wood-burning," Summit says. By turning the gourd upside down, it became a rose. The very deep initial carving was done with a round Kutzall bit, and the shaping detail was finished with various sizes of round and cylindrical cutting burrs. The stem and sepals were cut from the top of a thinner gourd. This has been left loose to help show this is really a gourd.

Tulip

A squirrel had chewed this thick gourd, but the remaining portion resembled the shape of a double-petal tulip just opening in the garden. The petals were shaped first with the coarse cylindrical sanding drum on a rotary carver and then finished with various shaping bits. The petals were shaped in the interior as well, and finally, stamens made of gourd stems were added deep inside the flower.

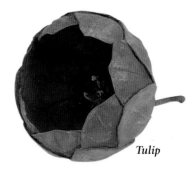

Tulip

Celtic Chain

The chain was carved into the neck of a canteen gourd and then burnished with gold paint and black polish to resemble an ancient chain resting on a blackened bowl.

Red, Red Rose. The sepals and stem are carved from a separate gourd. The rose petals were carved deeply into the shell. The dark stains between the petals emphasize the depth of the cuts. The entire gourd is protected with a thick coat of matte varnish.

Celtic Chain

SHAPED GOURDS

Ginger Summit

These gourds were inspired by carved wooden and ceramic vessels.

The gourds were divided into appropriate sections and lines drawn with a marking pen. (The graphite from pencils usually wears off during the lengthy process.)

"I did my initial carving with the coarse sanding drum or a cylindrically shaped Kutzall grinding bit. The edges of the sections were gradually sanded smooth with a fine-grit sanding drum. Final sanding was done by hand with many fine grades of sanding pads. I learned that it is very important during this process to work with gloves. Both the sanding pads and the gourd dust can be very irritating to the skin," Summit says. "I sealed and finished with leather dyes, wood stains, and many coats of wax."

A gourd being shaped during the sanding process.

Black Diamonds. This gourd was not grown in a mold or a net, but deeply carved into diamond shapes.

Gourd carved and sanded to accentuate vertical grooves.

Robert Fox

To begin a project, Robert Fox looks for unusually shaped gourds; then he designs a piece around the gourd, adding as little as possible to create a realistic appearance. He prefers gourds with relatively thin shells but ample thickness for his style of carving.

After determining how the gourd for his Swan naturally rests, he begins by marking a centerline, which acts as a reference point for doing the feather arrangement and determining head or tail position.

Swan

Detail of swan head.

Fox creates feather texture with a pneumatic tool.

Detail of curlew's feather layout and texture.

Curlew, fully textured bird.

A Gourd Carving Gallery

Flora Band

COMBINING CARVING TECHNIQUES & EMBELLISHMENT

This section contains samples of work by artists who combine many different techniques of carving with other kinds of embellishment to create complex designs of great beauty. The techniques are very different, but each artist has used vision and talent to transform the gourd into a unique work of art.

Don Weeke

Before he discovered gourds many years ago, Don Weeke was a basket maker. He has explored many different techniques and styles of carving gourds as well as unusual ways to combine them with natural materials, especially those from basketry.

He carves using the Dremel tool, with its many different sizes of cutter bits. After wood-burning the basic design outline on the gourd, Don often paints the exterior surface. Then when it is carved, the inner shell stands in pale contrast to the bold exterior. The inner shell may also be colored with a thinned acrylic paint, depending on the design.

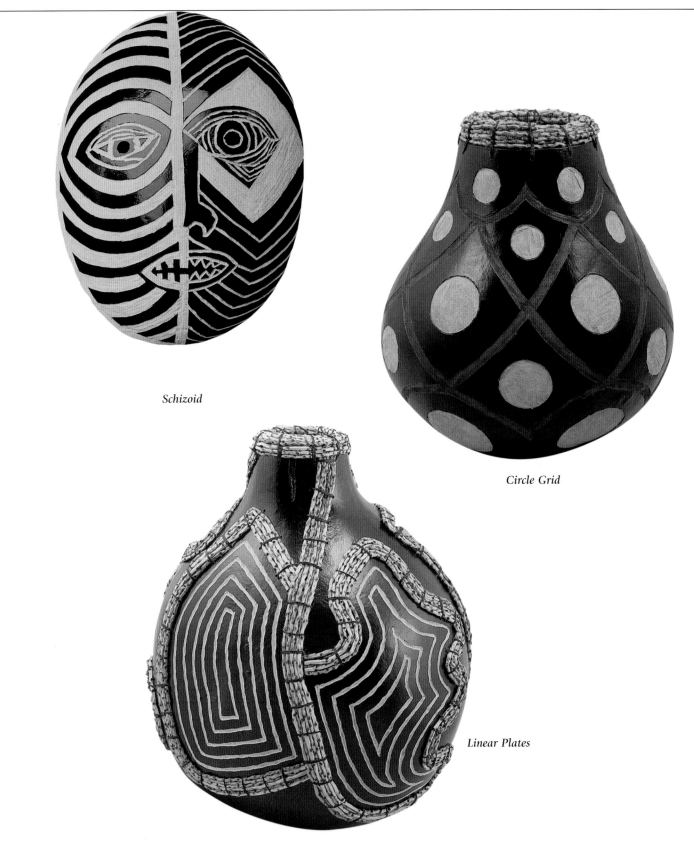

Schizoid

Circle Grid

Linear Plates

Gary Devine

Gary Devine is a fine draftsman, art teacher, and gourd pyro-engraver. He uses carving to enhance his works of art. To cut out the black latticework, he uses a MicroLux jigsaw. Then, in all areas to be painted in acrylic, he uses a 2-mm inverted vanadium cone burr to outline before clearing out a depth of about 2 mm with the 5-mm ball-tip. The gourd is inlaid with beads and abalone shell using the same technique. These relieved areas were then painted. Finally, the black areas of uncarved surface were painted.

Detail, Hollywood Style

Hollywood Style

Hollywood Style

Celtic Bowl

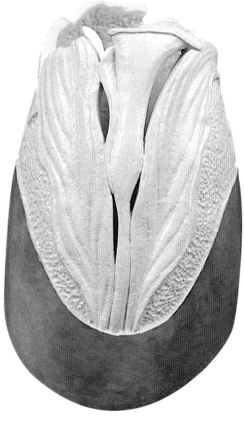

Calla Lily

Double Birds

Dr. Leslie Miller

Dr. Miller was a professor of mathematics. His daughter Marilyn Rehm grew gourds as she was growing up and amassed quantities of them in the storage shed. Eventually, Dr. Miller decided "to do something with them," and taking wood-carving tools from his workroom, he began creating unusual, innovative designs. A hallmark of Dr. Miller's work is that he uses only hand tools, and aside from natural wood stains, the gourds are not colored or otherwise embellished. The designs came from his own fertile imagination or illustrations that appealed to him and could be adapted to the unusual shape of a gourd.

One distinctive style that Dr. Miller initiated using gouges was a combination of stop-cut and sweep-through, which could be used with small gouges in random cuts to fill in empty spaces or in orderly rows to create the optical illusion of wavy lines.

Many of his gourds are divided into precise geometric shapes that interlock to cover the surface of the gourd completely. By alternately carving, dyeing the gourd, and then carving more design, he was able to create the impression of several layers or colors.

The idea of interlocking patterns is also seen in his fascination with the tessellation designs of the artist M. C. Escher.

Combining linear carving with a narrow-veiner gouge and removal of background, Dr. Miller created two memorable story gourds: Twelve Days of Christmas and Noah's Ark.

Generations of gourd carvers owe much to the inspiration of Dr. Miller and his family.

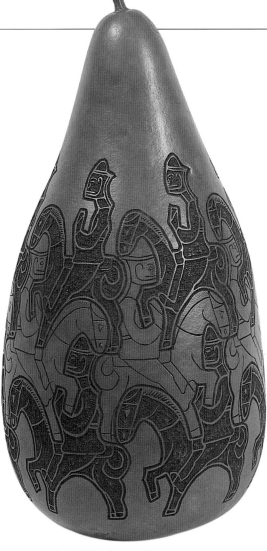

Medieval Warriors, with Escher pattern.

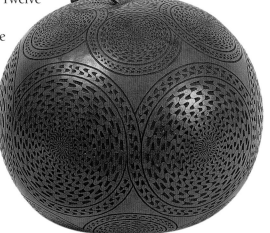

Circle Patterns

Twelve Days of Christmas

Noah's Ark

Seeing Stars. These 4x4 stars show the effect of alternating staining and carving to achieve a multidimensional effect.

Jan Seeger

Radial forms, rich color, and textures found in nature and the language of patterns—their rhythm, power, and movement—fascinate Jan Seeger. "My love of the natural environment inspires simplicity. I am also greatly influenced by traditional Pacific or Asian art forms and interested in employing traditional design and technique with contemporary materials, incorporating precious metals and exotic hardwoods," she says.

"My work process involves cleaning and cutting gourds into form; then a shape is created in which I establish a design and arrange a pattern. I set inlay material into the gourd shell by carving out a channel, using a Fordham rotary tool with a 5-mm knife-edge cutter to score, and a variety of round, cylinder, square, and small crosscut burrs to remove material. The pieces are then worked with leather dyes and finished with a hand-rubbed polish to convey a primitive feel."

Moana Nui

Korowhiti

Lidded Urn

Oko Hue

Denny Wainscott

Denny Wainscott describes his process: "Using a pencil, I draw the design on the gourd. Next I use the Detail Master wood-burning pen to burn the design into the piece. Then I use carbide burrs of many different sizes with the Paragraver air-turbine carver and carve away where I want my turquoise inlay and dark stain to be. After I complete the carving, I inlay the turquoise with epoxy. After the epoxy dries, I begin sanding with 150-grit sandpaper and work my way down to 2,000-grit wet sandpaper. To stain the gourd, I use a combination of Fiebing leather dyes and Minwax wood stains. After these dry, I seal the piece with an acrylic spray sealer. Next I carve away where I want the white inner layer of the gourd to show through. For this step, I prefer the Ultima engraver, again using a variety of carbide cutting burrs. Finally, I give the whole piece more coats of sealer." It's important to wear a good dust mask and have a strong dust-removal system in your work area.

Bear Heights. Photo by Denny Wainscott.

Dancing Deer. Photo by Denny Wainscott.

Sam Ponder

The whale-making process begins with the selection of the gourd, based on a combination of shape and thickness or durability. When the correct position for the gourd becomes apparent, Sam Ponder pencils in the dimensions and centers the various features, such as the blow hole, mouth line, eye and fin positions, and the symmetry of the rorqual throat grooves.

Ponder describes his technique: "Usually I begin the carving process by using the high-speed rotary carver with a carbide cutter on a flex shaft to cut the throat grooves, eyes, and blow holes. I then use the structured-tooth carbide cutter to make the vertical striations, which will be the baleen plates, followed by the grinding stone, which cleans up, and smoothes out the rough edges. I then open the gourd with a jigsaw. I carefully cut the mouth line around the baleen cuts, clean out the seeds, and scrape the interior of the gourd. This gives me the mouth hole and the two pieces of cutout gourd, which are then shaped and glued in under the upper lip to give the effect of baleen growing from the upper lip.

"I trace the fins and flukes onto another round gourd and cut them out with the jigsaw. Before assembling all the parts, I stain and seal them, and darken the interior of the cut gourd. After the carving and staining is done, I decide where I want the callosities (growths similar to deer antlers on the surface of the whale). Using a carbide cutter, I etch the darkly stained surface, which exposes the lighter colored material under the skin of the gourd. Although callosities usually extend outward, creating them in this way provides the contrast that's needed to set them off from the rest of the whale. Whales also have barnacles and all kinds of markings, so any kind of bump or gnarly spot on the gourd just adds to the texture.

"To attach the fins and flukes, I cut a notch into the surface of the gourd so that the glue will hold. When the glue is dried, it is colored with artist's oil and sealed with a spray polyurethane satin finish."

Humpback Whale

Humpback Whale

Hanging Whale

Right Whale

Bob Hosea

Bob Hosea, a wood turner, became very excited when he discovered that the gourds grown by Doug Welburn in Fallbrook, California, are thick enough to carve. Bob mounts the gourd on a lathe and rotates it at a moderate speed while holding a chisel against the shell. He can control the thickness of the gourd bowl and carve concentric grooves as well as bring out different textures and thicknesses of the gourd shell itself. He applies a sanding sealer to stiffen the fibers. Sanding the finished piece on the lathe with progressively higher grades of sandpaper and then waxing and buffing produces a finish that is hard to match by hand sanding.

Lathe-turned gourd. Black leather dye was applied before sealing, faint flame patterns were hand carved into the shell and then inlaid with clear InLace with gold flake added. Then it was waxed.

The concentric grooves are colored with permanent marker, then sealed and waxed.

Pat Boyd

Jewelry designer Pat Boyd became fascinated with the gourds her sister, Beverly Shamana, crafted. Following a trip to Africa, Boyd was haunted by memories of the African women's grace and their beautiful clothing. Her gourds were transformed into the mother, the dancer, and the woman immersed in daily activities. Boyd was able to use materials from her jewelry projects to turn each gourd into a work of art.

A Sense of Blessing

The Bag Lady, Carrier of Hope

Kathleen Kam

"The source of all that I create comes from centering energies through the *mana'o* of my being," Hawaiian artist Kathleen Kam says. "My choice to use many forms to express this connection cultivates in me a sense of place, of being Hawaiian, and connecting to the land. I was born and raised in Hawaii, and working with the *ipu* has given me patience, gratefulness, and humility. In the creation of all *pawehe*, great care is taken to ensure its longevity; therefore, a mixture of traditional and modern preparation techniques are applied to each hand-scrubbed gourd."

Her designs are carved freehand on the pre-painted gourd. She was a fine artist and teacher for 30 years.

"Electric tools are a must in the freehand 'drawing' style of carving, and bits used range from recycled dental bits of all sizes as well as medium to large tungsten and carbide ball-tip burrs," Kam says. "I begin the drawing first with a dental bit and work my way up to large bits and burrs to remove the negative space. A variable-speed transformer allows me to incise delicate to very sharp and deep cuts. I also use the *sgraffito* or scratchboard technique. First, I apply several layers of different tones of enamel paint. Then, using a very delicate touch with a dulled cutter, I remove single layers of paint to expose the different paint color underneath. I barely touch the color layer to achieve fine tonal differences in the carved areas as I strip or cut through layers of paint. All designs are based on native and endemic plants and flowers as well as our endangered native forest birds and marine life."

Kam uses colors minimally and applies them using an oil painter's style of glazing up to four layers. She varnishes all pieces upon completion.

He kumu lehua muimuia I ka manu, *the lehua tree, native to Hawaii, is depicted here covered with birds.*

He kumu lehua muimuia I ka manu. *This detail really shows the effectiveness of Kam's sgraffito technique of carving through one layer of colored enamel paint to reveal the colored enamel below it. This gives her carving tonal shading.*

Detail.

Ho'ola'inamanu ike aheahe. *"The birds pose quietly in the gentle breeze. They are at peace with the world, undisturbed and contented."*

Noho hele honu. *"Traveling turtle that stops briefly."*

Mark Doolittle

Each gourd piece features an inset fossil dating back 50 to 500 million years, which forms the central design element. Mark Doolittle says, "I then use hand-carving techniques to create flowing organic elements used to complement the inset fossil and integrate it into the surrounding gourd. I enjoy introducing large free-form negative spaces to introduce flow and interest and to create balance with the strong positive element of the fossil itself.

"My carving," Doolittle continues, "generally entails the use of ¼-inch spiral router bit, ⅛-inch and ¹⁄₁₆-inch straight carving burrs, and a small engraving ball-tip. The carving is finished with rasps, files, chisels, and sandpaper. No stains or dyes are used, although a clear sealer or resin protects the carving."

Fossil Trilobite #1

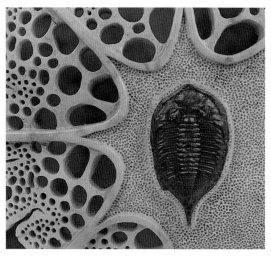

Fossil Trilobite #1 detail.

Fossil Ammonite

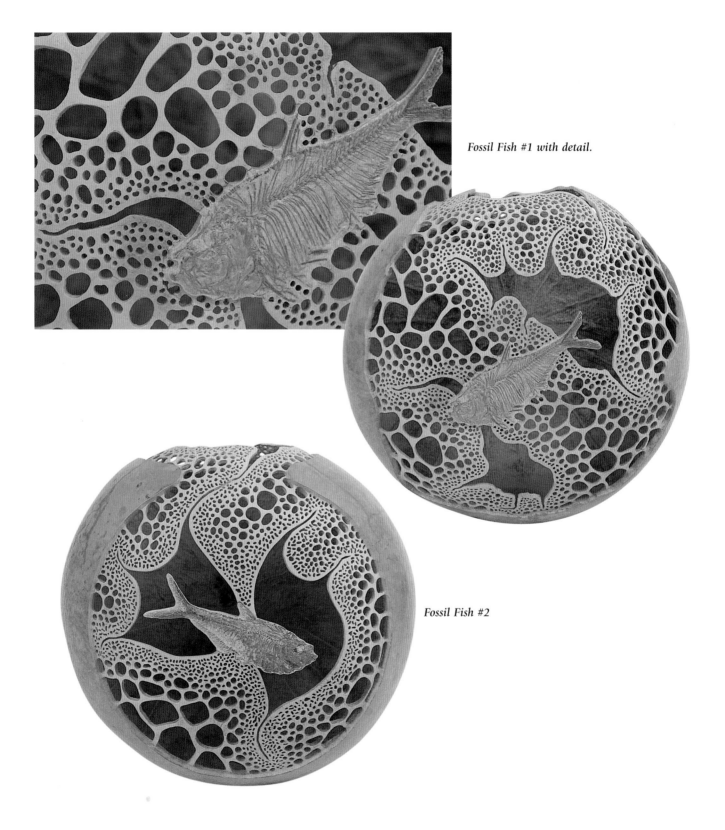

Fossil Fish #1 with detail.

Fossil Fish #2

Judy Cunningham

Judy Cunningham begins her carvings by first dyeing the gourd in her favorite Bismark brown and sometimes adding other colors. Her favorite part of the entire process is the design and composition. She begins laying out the design, starting at the bottom of the gourd, spiraling upward, and reserving a spot on the top for embellishment. Her favorite embellishment is her husband Larry's fused glass. Before she begins to carve, she puts on a thin layer of protective craft spray. Her preferred carving tool is the Fordham 350K air-turbine system using 1/16-inch diamond burrs.

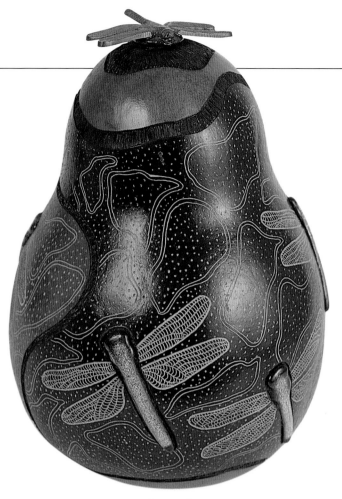

Dragonfly

Peacock

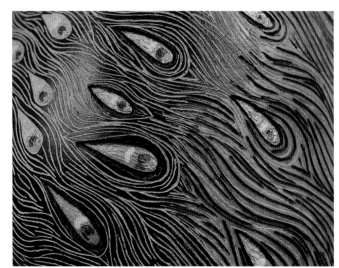

Peacock detail.

Zebras

Zebras details.

Creature

Bonnie Gibson

"For most of my gourds," Bonnie Gibson says, "I do the large, uncomplicated areas of carving with a Dremel tool. My favorite bits are a mini-saw burr (now discontinued), the inverted cone, and the ball-tip cutters. These are used for sand ripples and the basketry effects.

"For more detailed carving or to add texture, I use a Turbocarver II. I can carve for longer periods of time without fatigue using that tool because it is relatively lightweight and runs without heat buildup. In some cases, using this tool eliminates or reduces the amount of pyro-engraving needed to add texture to wildlife carving.

"I like the effect of different layers, so I try to add lower areas as well as raising areas with inlays of stone or other material, such as eggshell or beads. I also carve recesses into the gourd that I later fill with InLace. These areas are then ground smooth and polished after curing."

Bald Eagle

Bald Eagle, detail of turquoise inlay.

Snake Eye

Snail Swirls

Turquoise Fancies

Bear Trail

Denise Meyers

Based in part on an Egyptian necklace design, the piece Senruset's Necklace combines stone carvings and hieroglyphs on opposite panels. Denise Meyers created the gemstone inlay with turquoise, coral, malachite, and lapis.

"To make this piece, I first wood-burned the entire design with a Detail Master and then used the Dremel to carve away only those areas I wanted to inlay with gemstones. The Dremel allows me to remove the initial layer of skin with a small ball-tip, clean up the edges with a straight edge or very small ball-tip, and smooth the inner gourd surface with a diamond tip. I mix the gemstones with a two-part epoxy and fill the carved space, using a toothpick. After it is completely dry, I sand the excess inlay and epoxy off the gourd. Finally, I color the background with dyes and combinations of paints," Meyers says.

Senruset's Necklace

Senruset's Necklace, detail.

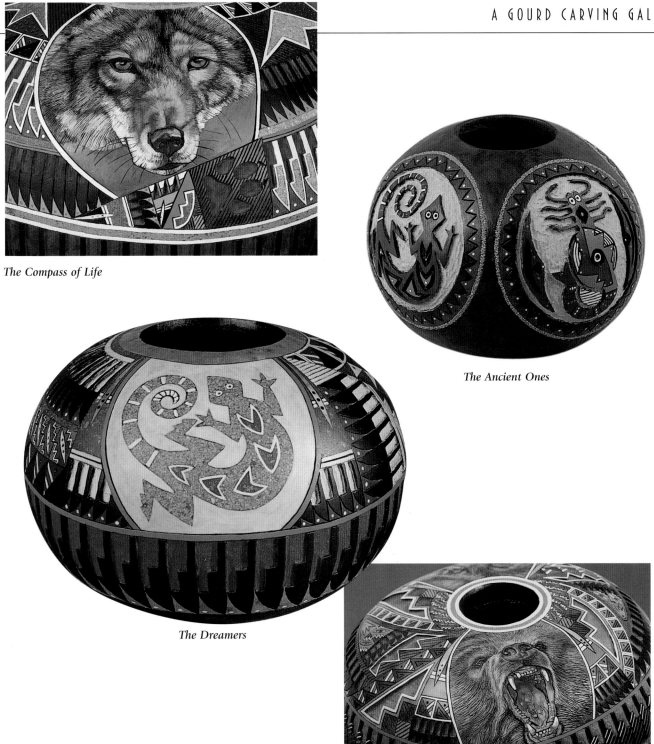

The Compass of Life

The Ancient Ones

The Dreamers

Yin and Yang

Gail Hohlweg

"In 1975, I saw a bronze pot in a Chinese exhibition. The bronze bean pot was made in the 11th century B.C. and was taken from tombs in western China in Anhwei province. This reproduction was constructed from five gourds. I penciled in the design and then burned in the details using the Razertip wood-burning pen. Then I carved the design, using #9, 5-mm 9-gouge; #11, 1-mm veiner; #11, 3-mm veiner; and #12 V parting tool. I finished the gourd with metallic paints to reproduce the antique surface," Gail Hohlweg says.

Oriental Bean Pot

Angela Briggs

Angela Briggs cuts bracelets from different shapes of gourds using a mini-saber saw or a hand hobby saw with 54 teeth per inch. For the actual carved patterns on the jewelry, she uses a ⅟₁₆-inch ball-tip cutter on a high-speed Dremel. After carving she dyes the gourd pieces, then polishes them. Sometimes she'll also use her Hot Tool with a circle tip or the side of the tool for designs. She also uses the side of her Razertip wood-burner to create different triangle shapes.

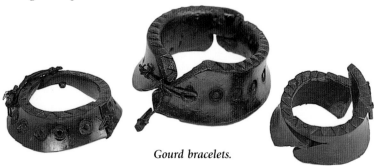

Gourd bracelets.

Gourd necklace.

CONTRIBUTING ARTISTS

Adams, Leigh
Alexander, Valene
Ames, Jeanne Lee
Arrigotti, Judy
Bernier, Latana Jan
Boland, Tim
Boyd, Pat
Briggs, Angela
Burtsfield, Dennis
Chapman, Jeanne
Cheeseman, Karen
Colligen, Bill
Comerford, Leah
Cunningham, Judy
Devine, Gary
Dillard, Robert
Doolittle, Kathy
Doolittle, Mark
Endicott, Eugene
Evaro, Linda
Finch, Betty
Forbes, Rhoda
Fox, Robert
Gates, Janis
Ghio, Rob
Gibson, Bonnie
Heineman, Gwen
Hohlweg, Gail

Holdsclaw, Terry
Hopkins, Lillian
Hosea, Bob
Iverson, Cass
Kam, Kathleen
Klopfenstein Kathi
Klopfenstein, Paul
Kusche, Thelma Dixie
Lee, Cindy
Leigh, Bonnie
Levesque, Susan
Lewis, Jerry
Lowry, Dege
Mangliers, Kris
Marcotte, Eileen
Martin, John
Matsutsuyu, Emiko
Medina, Tito
Merkle, Cam
Meyers, Denise
Miller, Leslie
Miller, Nancy
Mitchell, Ann
Molina, C. Siles
Muhly, Liza
Newick, Cyndee
Nigoghossian, Andre
Nong, Ban

Peckman, Whitney
 Johnson
Peterson, Dyan Mai
Ponder, Sam
Rehm, Marilyn
Reinhard, Walter
Ríos, Julio Seguil
Rittweger, Seth
Rizzi, John
Sairanen, Marcia
Schoon, Theo
Seeger, Jan
Segreto, Mary
Sheronda, Jai
Smith, Marguerite
Steiner, Julie
Stewart, Stella
Stone, Kemper
Strand, Jim

Swerdloff, Howard
Taylor, Shawn
Thomas, Noi
Thorp, Jack
Toth, Debra
Truman, Kimo
Turner, Gertrude
Wainscott, Denny
Walker, Jill
Wang, Julius
Weeke, Don
Williams, Bronii
Wiseman, Marshall
Wojeck, Mary
Wuttke, Ronna
Zhang Cairi
Zhang Gang
Zielinski, Lorraine

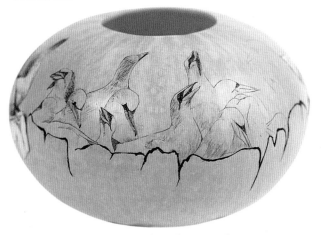

Scrimshaw bowl with birds, Gertrude Turner.

GUIDE TO HIGH-SPEED GRINDER BURRS & TIPS

These cutting tips come in many different diameters as well as textures. There are **stump cutters** with serrated edges; **solid carbide cutters**, which are fast cutting and leave a smooth finish; **texturing stones** for finer texturing; **fluted cutters** for areas where detail is important; **diamond cutters** for longer lasting bits; and **typhoon-style carbide burrs** for rapid removal of material. The photos show some of the basic shapes available.

This tree gourd from Brazil, like the Peruvian tree gourd, was also carved with much of the background removed around the design. Collection of Virginia Saunders.

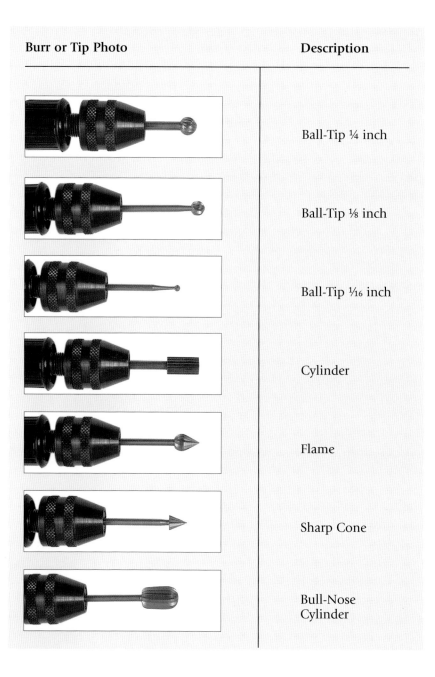

Burr or Tip Photo	Description
	Ball-Tip ¼ inch
	Ball-Tip ⅛ inch
	Ball-Tip ¹⁄₁₆ inch
	Cylinder
	Flame
	Sharp Cone
	Bull-Nose Cylinder

Burr or Tip Photo	Description
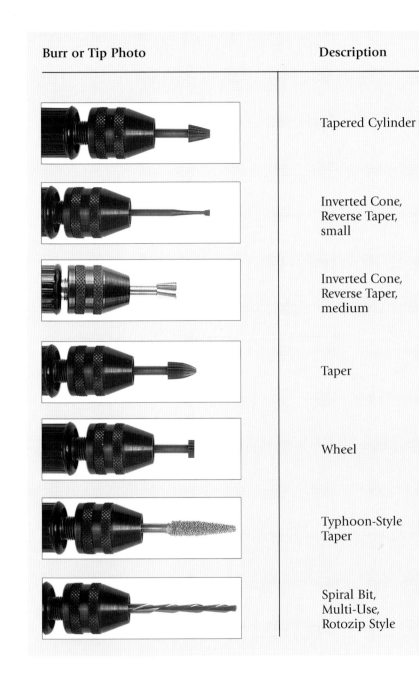	Tapered Cylinder
	Inverted Cone, Reverse Taper, small
	Inverted Cone, Reverse Taper, medium
	Taper
	Wheel
	Typhoon-Style Taper
	Spiral Bit, Multi-Use, Rotozip Style

Western Art Nouveau, Judy Cunningham

Lathe-turned gourd, Bob Hosea.

Lidded Potpourri, Ginger Summit

SUPPLY SOURCES

Many wood-carving supply stores, mail-order sources, and company websites have a wealth of listings and detailed information about particular carving tools. If you search the Web under the terms *wood carving* and *wood-carving tools,* you'll be busy for hours. The monthly magazine for wood carvers, *Chip Chats,* also contains dozens of ads for wood-carving tools.

Of course, when you are buying tools, first find out what kind of warranty comes with the tool, then determine who stands behind the warranty and how quickly you can have it repaired or get a replacement. Study the materials used in the tool's manufacture. Only then consider the selling price of the tool. An inexpensive tool with no follow-up service is really no bargain. Here are some popular brands gourd carvers used to create artworks in this book.

Hand-Carving Tools
Powergrip
Excel
X-acto

Power Carving Tools
Turbocarver II
Powercarver
Dremel
Fordham
Miyad Electric Carving System
Ultima
Paragraver
Proxxon
Strong 90 Micromotor

Miniature Jigsaws
Proxxon
MiniCraft
MicroLux
Gourd Saw

Wood-Burning Tools for Carving
Razertip
Optima
Detail Master
Colwood
Hot Tool

Gourds
American Gourd Society or local gourd
    chapters
Welburn Gourd Farm
Zittel Gourd Farm
Sandlady

Butterfly, Lorraine Zielinski

METRIC EQUIVALENTS

⅟₃₂ inch = 0.08 centimeters = 0.8 millimeters
⅟₁₆ inch = 0.16 centimeters = 1.6 millimeters
⅛ inch = 0.32 centimeters = 3.2 millimeters
¼ inch = 0.63 centimeters = 6.3 millimeters
½ inch = 1.25 centimeters = 12.5 millimeters
¾ inch = 1.9 centimeters = 19 millimeters
1 inch = 2.54 centimeters

1 foot = 30 centimeters
39 inches = 1 meter
1 cup = 8 fluid ounces = 240 milliliters
2 cups = 1 pint = 0.45 liter
4 cups = 2 pints = 1 quart = 0.89 liter
2 quarts = 1.9 liters
4 quarts = 1 gallon = 3.8 liters

Temperature Conversions

Fahrenheit to Centigrade (Celsius)
(Fahrenheit degrees − 32) × ⁵⁄₉ = Centigrade degrees
Centigrade (Celsius) to Fahrenheit
(Centigrade degrees × ⁹⁄₅) + 32 = Fahrenheit degrees

ACKNOWLEDGMENTS

We would like to thank the many artists who contributed gourd-carving artwork, methods, and techniques. We've been overwhelmed by the altruism of gourd artists who have generously shared their knowledge. Without their generous support, our book would have been slim. We especially want to thank Fernando Covarrubias for introducing us to Julio Sequil Ríos; and Paul Baumann and Bob Allen of Poco-a-Poco, for introducing us to Tito Medina. We are indebted to our families, Roger Summit, Sher Elliott-Widess, and Andy Widess, for their love, patience, and encouragement. And, of course, we thank those loyal folks at The Caning Shop, Shelly, Jenny, Andre, Lerryn, Tami, Patty, and Seth, who allowed us the time and the space to work and shoot photos.

Geometrics and Leaves,
Liza Muhly

INDEX

Additional Photo Credits

p. 1 (title page): Stars and Hexagons, Dr. Leslie Miller. Collection of Virginia Umberger and Sher Elliott-Widess.

p. 4: Figure Eight, Walter Reinhard

p. 5 (top): Falling Leaves, Cindy Lee

p. 24: Impressed gourd, Gourd Island Gourd Society, Liaoning, China.

p. 25 (top): Calabash bowl from Suriname, shows design impressed on interior surface. Collection of Ginger Summit.

p. 30: Fiddleheads, Karen Cheeseman

p. 31 (top): Sedentary, Karen Cheeseman

p. 34: Spiral-Cut Dipper, Jack Thorp

p. 35 (top): Spiral-Cut Round, Robert Dillard

p. 52: This Chinese engraved gourd was dyed and carved. Then the artist penned silver ink into the lines. Collection of Leigh Adams.

p. 53 (top): Peruvian Ploughman, Tito Medina. The light carved design stands in contrast to the dark dyed shell. The shell was first dyed, then carved.

p. 62: Melody, an Australian gourd. Collection of Virginia Saunders.

The gourd was first dyed, and then the very distinctive koala bear was carved. The light carved lines provide a good contrast against the darker shell.

p. 63 (top): Circle Dancers, Debra Toth

p. 78: Daisy Center, Ginger Summit. This chip-carved gourd uses traditional patterns.

p. 79 (top): Star-Flower Center, Ginger Summit

p. 88: Birdhouse, Walter Reinhard

p. 89 (top): Glittering Sun, Leah Comerford

p. 104: Flowers in Relief, John Martin

p. 105 (top): Geometric Band, Mary Segreto

p. 128: Connections, John Rizzi. Chipped Tibetan turquoise and opal inlays.

p. 129 (top): Pre-Columbian Kingfisher bowl, Cindy Lee. See other view on p. 134 (top).

p. 146: Master Saddlemaker, Betty Finch

p. 147 (top): Spiral Sculpture, Ginger Summit. The gourd was carved and sanded to accentuate spirals.